STRATEGIC INTUITION

STRATEGIC INTUITION

THE CREATIVE SPARK IN HUMAN ACHIEVEMENT

WILLIAM DUGGAN

Columbia Business School
Publishing

Columbia University Press
Publishers Since 1893
New York   Chichester, West Sussex
Copyright © 2007 Columbia University Press
All rights reserved

Library of Congress Cataloging-in-Publication Data
Duggan, William R.
Strategic intuition : the creative spark in human achievement / William Duggan.
    p.   cm.
Includes bibliographical references and index.
ISBN 978-0-231-14268-7 (cloth : alk. paper)
ISBN 978-0-231-51232-9 (e-book)
1. Creative ability in business.   2. Intuition.   3. Decision making.
4. Creative thinking.   I. Title.
HD53.D84 2008
153.3′5—dc22
2007019987

∞
Columbia University Press books are printed on permanent and
durable acid-free paper.
This book was printed on paper with recycled content.

Printed in the United States of America
c 10 9 8 7 6 5 4 3

References to Internet Web sites (URLs) were accurate at the time of writing. Neither
the author nor Columbia University Press is responsible for URLs that may have expired
or changed since the manuscript was prepared.

For Lynn and Emmaline

Contents

Preface   ix

1. Flash versus Blink
An Introduction to Strategic Intuition   1

2. Revolution on Earth
Flashes of Insight in Scientific Discovery   11

3. Two Halves of a Brain
Intelligent Memory in Neuroscience   25

4. Lieutenant M Saves Your Life
Expert Intuition in Action   37

5. The Corsican Conquers Europe
Coup d'Oeil in Classical Military Strategy   53

Contents

6. Warrior Buddha
The Path to Beginner's Mind   65

7. Gates and the Google Guys Go for It
Strategic Innovation in Business   79

8. Mouse, Minister, and Moneylender
The Art of What Works in Social Enterprise   113

9. Picasso Dines with an African Sculpture
Creative Combination in the Professions   143

10. Do We Do Dewey?
Teaching Strategic Intuition   159

11. Kennedy Shoots for the Moon
Progress Through Opportunity   171

Notes   179

Index   195

Preface

This book is the first full treatment of an idea I discovered some ten years ago. At that time I was one of many scholars applying our research expertise to the problem of economic development in poor countries. It began to dawn on me that my fellow experts had elaborate methods for analysis and planning that ignored or even contradicted the existing sources on how creative achievement really happens. Over time my informal inquiry into these sources turned into a more formal study that in turn led to this book.

In my inquiry, three authors stood out right away: Thomas Kuhn on scientific revolutions, Joseph Schumpeter on entrepreneurial leaps of progress, and Carl von Clausewitz on military strategy. It struck me that all three described similar mechanisms for creative advance in their fields. The implications of this similarity seemed enormous to me for other fields too, including my own. All three scholars had independently arrived at a universal description of the structure of human achievement.

Once I saw this common thread, I set out to translate it into practical concepts that fields beyond science, entrepreneurship, and war might understand and accept. For this step I joined the faculty of Columbia Business School. There I found fellow scholars in economics, sociology, psychology, and political science dedicated to translating research insights into practical applications for all kinds of management in business, government, and nonprofit organizations.

My own work fit right in. Even more, this rich research environment greatly expanded my horizon. Beyond Kuhn, Schumpeter, and von Clausewitz, I now found common ground in other domains as well, including neuroscience, psychology, business strategy, social enterprise, professional and artistic mastery, and even the self-help movement. It led me to a wider understanding of how to create useful ideas in any field, not just my own.

My early discoveries led to two preliminary statements of what I found.[1] Armed with these publications, I set out to teach what I learned as a graduate university course. Hundreds of students later, I am much wiser for it. I found my students quite open to the ideas I offered them but very demanding too. For the most part they aim for careers as practitioners, not scholars, so they served as a vivid stand-in for the development experts I first set out to inform. For them each idea has to have a practical implication for their own actions. Students at business schools these days go on to an astonishing range of fields—banking, the arts, social services, diplomacy, and virtually anything else you can think of. This range forced me to try to present my discoveries in their clearest and most universal form, for all kinds of human achievement.

The unifying idea of this book is a common mechanism at the heart of outstanding achievements in every domain of human endeavor. I call that mechanism "strategic intuition," although it goes by several other names in the various fields where I found it. Behind every story of major advance is a turning point where someone has a useful idea that changes the field or starts a new one. Strategic intuition explains what happens in the mind of whoever has that idea. For reasons I will discuss, you seldom read about exactly where a new idea came from. But once you do, again and again you find strategic intuition. And by understanding how it works, you can do it more and better yourself.

By the nature of its subject, this book spans so many fields that it deals with each one in a very summary manner. I do not claim mastery in these fields but only an understanding of how strategic intuition applies to them. Strategy itself is a mongrel field with no pure pedigree in any of the traditional academic disciplines. So too with this book. And the brevity of treatment of each field forces me to skip over many of the people and works of scholarship that have helped inform my thought. As a result I can name only some of the works I consulted as citations in the pages that follow. As for people, here I name just a few.

Marcia Wright of Columbia University taught me the value of history as an empirical discipline. Lynn Ellsworth, a fellow scholar in development, served as my first example of the proper blend of Kuhn, Schumpeter, and von Clausewitz in a field of action. A second example was Steve Kerr, chief learning officer first at General Electric and then at Goldman Sachs. When I discovered Steve and what he did, in a very real sense my main ideas came true.

At Columbia Business School, Ray Horton gave me a warm welcome and key counsel for translating theory into useful ideas for practitioners. Paul Glasserman helped me gain rapid exposure to the full range of creative faculty research and its practical implications. Amar Bhidé has taken up Schumpeter's mantle with his research on modern entrepreneurial achievement. And Dean Glenn Hubbard especially encouraged me to pursue the implications of my work for teaching strategy. Myles Thompson of Columbia University Press offered precious editorial guidance, as well as the prize chance to launch the new imprint of Columbia Business School Publishing. Marina Petrova of Columbia University Press worked myriad wonders on the manuscript itself.

Last but not least, my students at Columbia Business School contributed much to this work. It is no exaggeration to say that I learned as much from them as from all the scholarly sources

I consulted. The expression of an idea becomes the idea, and how I convey strategic intuition comes in large part from discussion with students. Our discussion continues online at www.strategic-intuition.com, where you are welcome to join in. If you do, I very much look forward to learning from you too.

STRATEGIC INTUITION

Flash versus Blink

An Introduction to Strategic Intuition

It's an open secret that good ideas come to you as flashes of insight, often when you don't expect them. It's probably happened to you—in the shower, or stepping onto a train, or stuck in traffic, falling asleep, swimming, or brushing your teeth in the morning.

Suddenly it hits you. It all comes together in your mind. You connect the dots. It can be one big "Aha!" or a series of smaller ones that together show you the way ahead. The fog clears and you see what to do. It seems so obvious. A moment before you had no idea. Now you do.

If this kind of flash of insight has ever happened to you, you're in very good company. It is the key element in some of the greatest achievements in human history: how Bill Gates founded Microsoft, how Picasso found his style, how the civil rights movement finally succeeded, how the Google guys conquered the Internet, how Napoleon conquered Europe, and so on through the ages. It's how innovators get their innovations, how artists get their creative ideas, how visionaries get their vision, how scientists make their discoveries, and how good ideas of every kind arise in the human mind.

In recent years neuroscience has made great strides in explaining how flashes of insight work. We find reference to flashes of insight as well in a variety of older fields that seek to explain how good ideas for action happen. They appear in Asian philosophy, classical military strategy, business strategy, the history of science, and the newer field of cognitive psychology. By pulling together these various sources, we are able to arrive at a modern discipline that puts flashes of insight at the center of a philosophy of action across all fields of human endeavor.

I call this new discipline *strategic intuition*. It is very different from ordinary intuition, like vague hunches or gut instinct. Ordinary intuition is a form of emotion: feeling, not thinking. Strategic intuition is the opposite: it's thinking, not feeling. A flash of insight cuts through the fog of your mind with a clear, shining thought. You might feel elated right after, but the thought itself is sharp in your mind. That's why it excites you: at last you see clearly what to do.

Strategic intuition is also different from snap judgments. These are technically *expert intuition*, a form of rapid thinking where you jump to a conclusion when you recognize something familiar. In *Blink* (2005), Malcolm Gladwell brought decades of research on expert intuition to the attention of a wide audience.[1] This book attempts something similar for strategic intuition. Expert intuition is always fast, and it only works in familiar situations. Strategic intuition is always slow, and it works for new situations, which is when you need your best ideas.

This difference is crucial, because expert intuition can be the enemy of strategic intuition. As you get better at your job, you recognize patterns that let you solve similar problems faster and faster. That's expert intuition at work. In new situations your brain takes much longer to make enough new connections to find a good answer. A flash of insight happens in only a moment, but it may take weeks for that moment to come. You can't rush it. But your expert intuition might see something familiar and make a snap judgment too soon. The discipline of strategic intuition requires you recognize when a situation is new and turn off your expert intuition. You must disconnect the old dots, to let new ones connect on their own.

The term *strategic intuition* distinguishes this discipline from other forms of intuition and also places it firmly in the field of strategy. Classical texts on strategy from Asia give us our first rough sketches of how flashes of insight work, especially the *Bhagavad Gita* from India (400 B.C.), Sun Tzu's *The Art of War* from China (450 B.C.), and Miyamoto Musashi's *Book of Five Rings* from Japan (1645).[2] These works apply Hindu, Tao, and Zen Buddhist philosophy to the problem of military strategy. The formal science of strategy begins with classical European military texts, especially *On War* by Carl von Clausewitz (1832), and here too flashes of insight reign.[3]

The European version of strategy spread from the military to business in the late nineteenth century and then to government, nonprofit agencies, and professions at large in the twentieth century. Wal-Mart has a strategy, your state department of health has a strategy, the Girl Scouts have a strategy, and so do doctors and lawyers and every other modern profession. But as strategic ideas spread from the military, flashes of insight were lost in translation. The leading ideas in strategy today leave them out completely. For example, in the 1980s Michael Porter's *competitive strategy* became the reigning paradigm in business. It tells you how to analyze your own strategy in light of your industry and your competitors. But it does not tell you how to come up with a strategic idea: that's a creative step Porter leaves out. Strategic intuition, in contrast, puts the strategic idea itself at the center of strategy. That makes it the first major breakthrough in the field of strategy in over twenty years.

The purpose of this book is to show how the discipline of strategic intuition works. In the first half of the book we study the theory of strategic intuition in its original forms: the history of science, neuroscience, cognitive psychology, European military strategy, and Asian philosophy. In the second half we learn how to apply strategic intuition in business, in social programs, in professions of all kinds, and in education. Along the way we overturn conventional wisdom about strategic planning, the scientific method, creativity, imagination, rational decision making, teamwork, leadership, innovation, brainstorming, and the divide between the "hard" and "soft" skills of science and art.

The leading notions in all these arenas arose at a time before modern neuroscience was able to show how ideas really happen in the mind. They all preserve a distinction between two kinds of mental activity: rational thought and creative imagination. In that old model the only thing that brings the two sides together is teamwork, where you're rational and I'm creative and together we can be both. But strategic intuition as a discipline combines both abilities in the same mind, through flashes of insight large and small. Understanding that can change to some degree how you plan and organize actions of every kind.

Strategic intuition also puts active use of the human mind back at the center of human achievement. Flashes of insight lie at the heart of great achievements of all kind throughout history. But they usually hide in plain sight, because accounts of what happened typically leave them out. Instead, for example, you read that social, political, and economic forces were ripe for the rise of someone like Napoleon. Or you read that the circumstances and events of Napoleon's childhood and early youth, combined with his innate character, gave him the personal traits that fueled his climb from corporal to emperor in just ten years. Instead of Napoleon we might plug in Bill Gates—or any other modern hero—and the message is still the same.

Both these explanations of human achievement—external forces beyond your control and inner traits of character—give us little guidance for our own lives. Either the world around you will propel you to greatness, like Napoleon or Gates, or it won't. There's nothing you can do about it. Or you are who you are and you can't change that, and nothing you've done so far shows that you have what it takes for greatness. External forces or inner traits have already sealed your fate. In contrast, strategic intuition shows how flashes of insight leap beyond the forces around you and who you are within them. The idea for action that a flash of insight gave to Napoleon or Gates was not the inevitable result of historical forces or of innate character or talent. The flash of insight fits your time and who you are—that's part of why it's a good idea, not a bad one. But no one can predict what that flash of insight will be. The individual human mind always stands at the center of how great achievements happen.

Although the discipline of strategic intuition rightly belongs in the field of strategy, it brings together elements from other disciplines as well. That is because it deals above all with concrete reality, not abstract theory. Scholarly fields arise as attempts by human beings to organize knowledge about the world in ways that other humans can understand. They are never full and true pictures of the world itself. That's why Einstein drew on many fields for his theory of relativity, and Marie Curie won the Nobel Prize twice, in chemistry and physics. And so on through history, to Bill Gates, the Google guys, and beyond. Scholarly disciplines are excellent ways to organize knowledge, but don't mistake them for the real world.

This book presents each discipline in turn, for what it can contribute to our understanding of strategic intuition. That makes the book eclectic in the extreme. The first half of the book covers five scholarly fields that help explain how flashes of insight work in theory: the history of science, neuroscience, cognitive psychology, military strategy, and Asian philosophy. The second half covers four fields that apply strategic intuition in practice: business, social enterprise, the professions, and education. In each case we see how flashes of insight apply to the methods for action that rule that field.

In this way, strategic intuition becomes like a cottage you come upon in the middle of a forest. You move up close, look around the outside, and then peer through each window to see what's inside. Each window gives you a different view of the same thing. You look in one window, then another, then another, and then at the end you find you're inside the cottage. It all comes together in your mind. You understand strategic intuition.

Our first scholarly field is the history of science. Many of the world's greatest achievements are scientific. For example, the scientific revolution took us out of the Middle Ages and into the modern world. And science gives us the world's most respected method for coming up with useful ideas: the scientific method. Most professions—law, business, and myriad others—try to emulate the scientific method in their own fields. So right away we ask, Does strategic intuition conform to or violate the scientific method? To answer that question we turn to Thomas Kuhn, the great historian of scientific achievement. In *The Structure of Scientific Revolutions* (1962) Kuhn gives us a blow-by-blow account of how science really advanced, in the period from Copernicus to Einstein.[4] Sure enough, we find flashes of insight at the very heart of it. The result is a new understanding of the scientific method, where strategic intuition stands out as one of its major steps.

Our second field is neuroscience. We trace the history of two Nobel Prizes, to Roger Sperry in 1981 and Eric Kandel in 2000. Sperry won for his work on the two-sided brain: the right side is creative and intuitive but irrational, and the left side is rational and analytical but lacks imagination. Sperry studied actual patients with their brains cut in half. This left–right idea spread around the world and remains strong to this day. Someone will say, "I'm a left-brained type," or "Let's use our right brains on this." In the Sperry model strategic intuition would be impossible, as it combines both sides of the brain. And so enters Kandel, who overturns Sperry with a whole-brain model that combines analysis and intuition in all modes of thought. Neuroscientists call it *intelligent memory*, where flashes of insight large and small take past elements from memory anywhere in the brain and combine them in new ways. This new model reveals strategic intuition as a form of rational thought in the whole brain, rather than irrational thought on the irrational side of the brain.

For our third field, psychology, we study expert intuition—the snap judgments of experts in action. The psychologist Gary Klein pioneered the study of rapid decision making in real-life situations, starting at a firehouse in Cleveland. An emergency call, a torn artery, and the swift actions of Lieutenant M, the officer in charge, led Klein to understand how snap judgments combine past elements in the expert's mind without any conscious thought. They just happen, from practice. Our study of expert intuition takes intelligent memory out of the neuroscience laboratory and into real life. This sets the stage for future chapters, where we see how strategic intuition applies the same mental mechanism as expert intuition, but more slowly, more consciously, and in new situations where past expertise is not enough. Expert intuition works for familiar situations—you get better and faster at your job. But strategic intuition works for the unfamiliar, where every strategic situation is different to some degree.

Our next field is classical military strategy. The word *strategy* entered the English language in 1810, when scholars first turned the subject into a formal discipline of study. From there, strategy spread to business in the late nineteenth century and to other fields in the twentieth. The first great work of strategy scholarship, von Clausewitz's *On War*, put flashes of insight at the fore of how good generals think. Von Clausewitz gives us key elements that accompany a flash of insight: examples from history, which you must already have in mind; presence of mind, where you expect the unexpected and don't prejudge which examples you will draw on; the flash of insight itself, which selects and combines the right examples; and resolution, where you follow through despite the uncertainties and obstacles ahead. These four elements solve the problem of how intelligent memory applies to unfamiliar situations: the elements you draw on come from the past, but their combination is something new.

From classical European military strategy we move to classical Asian military strategy. Half the world lives in countries where the leading ideas about thinking for action come not from American or European scientists and scholars but from the ancient traditions of India and China. Elements of classical philosophy from these countries show a striking similarity to the four steps of von Clausewitz. These traditions pay special attention to presence of mind: the mental discipline of freeing your thoughts to let the flash of insight come. Asian martial arts apply this discipline to military strategy in a way we can recognize as strategic intuition.

Our next field is business strategy. We tell the story of the computer revolution in the same way that Kuhn told the story of the scientific revolution. From Gates to Google, via IBM and Apple, we trace each great achievement as strategic intuition in action. We then look to the reigning models of business strategy to see what they say about the same subject. Sure enough, they leave out how strategists actually come up with their ideas. For that we must go back to Joseph Schumpeter, an economist of the 1940s who explained leaps in business achievement in terms we now recognize as strategic intuition. We find a way to reconcile Schumpeter's work with modern models of strategy, including Porter and financial models that planners use to project a strategy into the future.

Our next field is social enterprise. This is a new name for an old idea: applying elements of management science to government and nonprofit agencies. Strategy is one of those elements, for every organization needs a strategy. Here we tell the story of three great social movements—civil rights in the United States, how American women won the right to vote, and microfinance in poor countries—as strategic intuition in action again. We then see how strategic intuition conflicts with reigning ideas of how agencies think they should make their strategy. We also apply a tool from the business world—the insight matrix from General Electric—to show how to use strategic intuition as a standard procedure in any organization. This cuts against a recent trend toward rigorous post-program evaluations that claim to apply the scientific method to social problems. As Kuhn shows us, the real scientific method works by strategic intuition.

Next come the professions. Chief among them are law and medicine, but any practical education or experience makes you a member of a professional field: engineering, journalism, social work, international development, information technology, media—the list goes on and on. In most professions you don't make quick decisions like Klein's firefighters, yet you seldom think about strategy. Instead you master your field as an expert, and then you get creative. That's where strategic intuition comes in. Creative ideas in a professional field—even the arts—arise the same way they do in science. This contrasts sharply with brainstorming, where you rely on pure imagination. But the scientific method depends not on imagination but on discovery, through strategic intuition. You do not imagine the unknown. You discover it and make it known. And it turns out to be different from what you imagined.

Our last field is education. This book presents strategic intuition as its own discipline, but each field of knowledge should teach its own version in its regular course of instruction. Lawyers should learn strategic intuition for lawyers, doctors for doctors, artists for artists, and so on. And shouldn't you start in grade school? A century ago John Dewey launched a progressive education movement that claims to impart creative thinking skills beyond the traditional disciplines. And in graduate education the Harvard case method follows this progressive tradition. Yet a closer look at this tradition shows that it misses a key element that makes flashes of insight possible: examples from history to put on the shelves of your brain and combine. Methods that teach such examples offer a better education for strategic intuition.

Before you turn the page and look through the first window of the cottage, I'd like to give a warning. As you see how great achievements really happen, your first reaction might be disappointment. It's like what happens to the audience at a magic show when someone pulls back the curtain to reveal the magician's tricks. It pricks our balloon. The mystery is gone. If that's what Bill Gates did—or Picasso or Einstein—then what's the big deal? But like that same audience, instead we might start to think: if that's how it works, with enough practice we can do it too. And that's exactly the point. I hope these examples inspire you in that way. Strategic intuition puts leaps of human achievement within the grasp of all human beings—of people like you.

2

Revolution on Earth

Flashes of Insight in Scientific Discovery

In the late spring of 1543, the great astronomer Nicolaus Copernicus lay on his deathbed in Frombork, Poland. He was seventy-one years old, paralyzed on his right side, and failing fast in sight and mind. His followers brought straight from the press the first printed copy of his life's work, *On the Revolutions of Celestial Orbits*. On that same day, May 24, Copernicus died.

That deathbed book launched the scientific revolution. The laws of science came to replace the hand of God as the moving force in the workings of nature. Nearly a century and a half after Copernicus, the scientific revolution came to a close when Isaac Newton published his *Mathematical Principles of Natural Philosophy* in 1687. From then on, science reigned over theology in the academies of Europe. These bookends of the scientific revolution—Copernicus's *Revolutions* and Newton's *Principles*—still stand as the two greatest landmarks in the progress of science through the ages.

The scientific revolution brought forth a long list of specific achievements, from Copernicus in astronomy to Newton in physics. It also gave us the world's most respected method for coming up with useful ideas: the scientific method. If the laws of science rule nature, the scientific method is the way to discover them. The scientific method is so successful that most professions these days—law, business, and many others—try to emulate it. And so we ask: Does strategic intuition violate the scientific method?

If the scientific method can solve problems in so many fields, perhaps strategy is just one more way of solving problems. Instead of applying strategic intuition to strategy, why not apply the scientific method?

To answer this question we turn to *The Structure of Scientific Revolutions*, where Thomas Kuhn gives us a blow-by-blow account of how scientific achievement really happens.[1] Kuhn began as a physicist in the 1950s but then switched to the history of science when he discovered how past achievements in physics actually came about. Each new generation of scientists typically skips over the details of how exactly one set of ideas gave way to another. First, scientists believed one thing, and then they believed another. It was Kuhn's great contribution to pin down the precise steps of how scientists in general, and Copernicus in particular, make the leap from one idea to the next.

Throughout this book we will ask the same question—Exactly how did it happen?—about other leaps of human achievement. If we ourselves want to contribute to major advances in our own fields, we might do well to study how others did it before us. We start with the story of how Copernicus made his achievement and then proceed to what Kuhn concluded from that story. From there we see how Kuhn generalized beyond Copernicus to other scientific advances, and then what we might carry over to other forms of human endeavor. What Kuhn describes is very different from conventional wisdom on how the scientific method works. Instead, we will learn that it is strategic intuition.

Let's start with Copernicus himself, the first great figure of the scientific revolution. What kind of revolutionary was he? We might expect him to be an atheist, or at least a nonbeliever, or even a religious dissident. When Copernicus was in his forties, Martin Luther posted his 95 Theses on the door of a church in Wittenburg, in neighboring Germany, using the same Latin that Copernicus wrote in. Religious upheaval was on the way. But we have no evidence of Copernicus as an enemy of the Catholic Church, like Luther. Quite the contrary. In his twenties Copernicus became a canon of the Catholic cathedral at Frombork. He held that position all his life.

A canon was a religious official who performed a variety of professional duties, for pay, in the vast bureaucracy that the Church maintained across Europe. Some canons were also priests, but we have no record of whether Copernicus was one of them. He administered Church property and affairs with particular specialty in law and finance. In his spare time he took up astronomy, including one puzzle that weighed on Church officers all the way up to the pope: the religious calendar.

Despite enormous progress in astronomy through the ages, scholars could not specify the exact date of religious holidays. Existing calendars relied on the moon and sun, but the precise relation of these heavenly bodies to a calendar year eluded astronomers. The cycle of the year did not fit exactly a full number of suns or moons—that is, days or lunar months.

Copernicus studied under noted astronomers at universities in Krakow and Bologna. In 1514 the Church-wide Lateran Council consulted him on the calendar question, but for Copernicus the problem of the sun and moon quickly turned into the larger mystery of the planets. Over the millennium and a half that came before, astronomers made great progress in plotting the course of all the heavenly bodies they could see with the naked eye, except for seven: the sun, moon, Mercury, Venus, Mars, Jupiter, and Saturn. While all other heavenly bodies made elegant circles through the sky, these seven wandered in odd paths, sometimes doubling back in patterns very different from each other. The word *planet* means "wanderer" in ancient Greek. Before Copernicus astronomers thought the sun and moon were planets too.

There were three categories of astronomical objects current at the time: first, the earth, at the center of the universe; second, the heavenly bodies arrayed around the earth; and third, the planets, a special category of heavenly body. In the days before the telescope, astronomers had no way of knowing that the sun and stars were made of fire and that the earth, moon, and planets rock.

They were all just points of light in the sky, with the sun the biggest of all.

Ptolemy of Alexandria, who died around A.D. 165, led the way in plotting the circles of heavenly bodies around the earth. For the wandering planets Ptolemy plotted similar circles but added circles within circles at various points to approximate the odd path of each planet, including the moon and sun. The formulas were both different from planet to planet and not very accurate for predicting each position. After Ptolemy, the formulas grew more and more elaborate, but they did not resolve the problem. Months and years depended on the moon and sun, which the Ptolemaic formulas failed to match up with enough accuracy to specific days of the year.

For his breakthrough, Copernicus brought together three elements available to all his fellow astronomers. First, he took the idea that the earth moves around the sun rather than the reverse from Aristarchus, a well-known Greek astronomer who died around 230 B.C. Second, he used data on observations of heavenly bodies that astronomers had built up since Ptolemy's time. Third, he applied advances in trigonometry from recent centuries. It was a new combination of existing elements: Copernicus used advanced trigonometry on Ptolemy's data to test Aristarchus's idea.

In this light, the Copernican revolution seems more like a minor uprising. He was the first to apply trigonometry, which he did not invent, to someone else's idea, using data he did not compile. And his attitude to the Church comes through in his Preface:

> To The Most Holy Lord, Pope Paul III:
>
> I began to chafe that philosophers could by no means agree on any one certain theory of the mechanism of the Universe, wrought for us by a supremely good and orderly Creator. . . . [I]t is to your Holiness rather than to anyone else that I have chosen to dedicate these studies of mine, since in this remote corner of Earth in which I live you are regarded as the most eminent by virtue

along of the dignity of your Office and of your love of letters and science.... Mathematicians ... will hold that these my labors contribute somewhat even to the Commonwealth of the Church, of which your Holiness is now Prince.... What results I have achieved therein, I leave to the judgment of learned mathematicians and of your Holiness in particular.[2]

Copernicus's book was hardly a declaration of revolution like Luther's 95 Theses. It was a memo to the boss. His solution to the calendar problem did not deny the hand of God but gave that hand a more fitting and orderly design. Certainly Copernicus's Preface might help him avoid the charge of blasphemy, but there is no evidence that he considered his work a threat to the Church. Sure enough, the earth did not shake when the book came out. Copernicus passed away quietly, and astronomers discussed his findings. Some of his calculations ended up forty years later in Pope Gregory's revised Church calendar, which most of the world still uses today.

Kuhn says that the relation of the earth to the sun—which Copernicus took from Aristarchus—was his only break with the Ptolemaic tradition:

The cosmological frame in which his astronomy was embedded, his physics, terrestrial and celestial, and even the mathematical devices that he employed to make his system give adequate predictions are all in the tradition established by ancient and medieval scientists.[3]

Kuhn goes on to explain that a breakthrough is part of both the past it came from and the future it starts, in the same way that a bend in the road serves as the end of one direction and the beginning of another. You can stand at the bend and look back to where the road came from and then turn to see where it goes. But if you stand elsewhere on the road, you see either a straight line that ends at the bend or a straight line that began at the same bend.

Only at the point of breakthrough can you see both directions at once. The future comes from the past, but not in a straight line.

The route from Copernicus to Newton passes through Kepler, Galileo, and numerous other scientists whose contributions mirror on varying scales what Kuhn tells us about Copernicus's own breakthrough. Because he came at the end of the scientific revolution, Newton owed the greatest debt to other scientists. He admitted as much when he wrote, "If I have seen farther, it is by standing on the shoulders of giants." Each revolutionary brought a new combination of existing elements to bear at a particular time. At the exact moment of their achievement, though, they hardly look revolutionary at all.

Kuhn's notion of a bend in the road is a striking contrast to the common idea of a breakthrough as a leap in progress, where there's a break in the road and you leap over the gap. Through bends rather than breaks in the road, Kuhn keeps our feet very much on the ground. The common idea of how a leap of progress happens is a leap of imagination. Kuhn gives us an alternative to imagination that we can apply to realms of achievement other than science. He shows us in detail how the bend in the road happens: a selective combination of elements from the past makes something new. The elements themselves are not new. Aristarchus plus Ptolemy plus trigonometry equals the Copernican revolution.

From his work on Copernicus, Kuhn generalized to scientific advance in general. *The Structure of Scientific Revolutions* offers a long list of similar examples: Franklin, Darwin, Volta, Lavoisier, Maxwell, Cavendish, Boyle, Coulomb, Priestley, Roentgen, Scheele, and Black, to name just a few. He calls each bend in the road a "paradigm shift" where scientists switch from one set of theories, methods, questions, training, careers, terminology, and problems to another. In "normal" science, as from Ptolemy to Copernicus, a single paradigm dominates the field. In "revolutionary" science a new paradigm emerges in embryonic form and, over time, competes on all those dimensions with the reigning paradigm.

When enough scientists from the first paradigm die off or convert, and enough young scientists grow up in the new paradigm, the shift occurs. The new paradigm wins. It now becomes the old paradigm. Later, a new paradigm emerges to challenge it. And so the pattern continues through the ages.

In other fields, we can usually recognize the equivalent of a scientific paradigm. In business we call it a business model. In art we call it a style. The military calls it a doctrine. In religion it's a belief system. And so on through the various branches of human endeavor. Sometimes one dominant paradigm kills off the others. Elsewhere they coexist: bookstores and Amazon.com, opera and Broadway musicals. But in all fields, paradigms still come and go, even when it's not winner-take-all.

We saw that Copernicus's achievement was a gradual one, from elements that already existed. But he did not come up with a new theory of physics. The new theory followed, with Newton, at the end of the scientific revolution. This sequence for a paradigm shift—achievement, then theory—is exactly backward from common ideas on how progress happens. In the typical notion of the scientific method, first you posit a theory, and then you conduct an experiment to test it. If your experiment works, you have an achievement. The sequence is theory, then achievement—exactly opposite to how the scientific revolution happened.

That was Kuhn's whole point. He overturned the conventional wisdom on how science works. His main question in *Structure* was this:

Why is the concrete scientific achievement, as a locus of professional commitment, prior to the various concepts, laws, theories, and points of view that may be abstracted from it?[4]

In the Copernicus example, the overall paradigm shift that the scientific revolution made was from Aristotle's *Physics*, dating from around 350 B.C., to Newton's physics. Copernicus's system was the turning point. But his theory of physics fit Aristotle's, not Newton's. Copernicus provided the achievement—Aristarchus plus trigonometry plus Ptolemaic data equaled the solar system—and Newton provided the theory. Copernicus had no theory, other than the Creator's hand: he did not explain why the earth goes around the sun. He just showed that it did. In the same way scientists discovered oxygen before they knew what it was. And so on through countless other scientific discoveries. The achievement precedes the theory.

This simple reversal of sequence yields a very different scientific method from what you learned in elementary school. Your teacher told you to start with a hypothesis. Then you design an experiment to test it. Then you observe the results. You reject or accept the hypothesis. If you reject it, you start again with another. But this is the experimental method, not the scientific method. The experimental method is part of the scientific method, but it's not the first step. Scientists first have to figure out what hypothesis to test. That's usually the most important part.

Let's hear from Roger Bacon, the first scholar in Europe to write about the scientific method. At Oxford University he studied under perhaps the first true laboratory scientist of the Middle Ages, Robert Grosseteste. In his *Opus Majus* of 1267, Bacon wrote:

> At first one should believe those who have made experiments or who have faithful testimony from others who have done so . . . experience follows second, and reason comes third.[5]

Step 1 of the scientific method is: look in the laboratories of other scientists. Step 2 is your own experiments, or "experience" as Bacon calls it. Step 3 is your reason. In the real scientific method, the hypothesis comes third, not first, as a product of your reason. Descartes contributed to the misunderstanding of the proper sequence with his *Discourse on Method* of 1637. He makes science seem like an act of reasoning about your observations of the natural world. Observation and reason are certainly important to science, but the achievements of other scientists come first. Scientists borrow from other scientists as the first step in their own discoveries, over and over, down through the ages.

We saw how achievement precedes theory in the shift from Aristotle's physics to Newton's, via Copernicus. It was certainly true as well of the next great shift in the same field, from Newton to Einstein. The achievements that Einstein brought together in 1905 as the theory of relativity came from a variety of scientists in a variety of branches of physics, especially from Maxwell, Poincaré, and Lorentz. For example, in 1900 Poincaré advanced his "principle of relativity," with two key elements that Einstein took up: "1. There is no absolute space. . . . 2. There is no absolute time."[6] And the winner of the Nobel Prize in 1911, Wilhelm Wein, proposed both Lorentz and Einstein for the Nobel Prize in 1912. Neither won. (It went instead to Nils Dalén "for his invention of automatic regulators for use in conjunction with gas accumulators for illuminating lighthouses and buoys.")

So scientific advance does not come about by a leap of thought to a new theory, but rather from combining specific achievements that lead to a theory, which explains them. It's an act of combination, not imagination. Specifically, it's the selective recombination of previous elements into a new whole. Pieces of the past come together to make a new future. But how does that recombination happen, exactly?

Here Kuhn posits "flashes of intuition" as the mechanism at work. This is different from "deliberation and interpretation"—that is, the leap does not come about simply by thinking hard. Instead, scientists speak of "scales falling from their eyes," a "lightning flash," or that "the relevant illumination comes in sleep."[7] The most famous example is Newton: legend tells us an apple fell on his head, and that gave him his flash of insight on gravity. In truth Newton saw an apple fall—it did not hit him—but the story conveys the basic idea that leaps of thought come about by flashes of insight.

Kuhn spoke from experience. He had his own breakthrough on his life's work as just such a flash of insight. He remembered the moment exactly. For weeks he had been poring over Aristotle, struggling to understand how someone so brilliant, observant, and meticulous could be so completely wrong, and how countless equally brilliant scientists through the ages had actually agreed with him. And then:

> I was sitting at my desk with the text of Aristotle's *Physics* open in front of me and with a four-colored pencil in my hand. Looking up, I gazed abstractedly out the window of my room—the visual image is one I still retain. Suddenly the fragments in my head sorted themselves out in a new way, and fell into place together. My jaw dropped, for all at once Aristotle seemed a very good physicist indeed, but of a sort I'd never dreamed possible. Now I could understand why he had said what he said, and what his authority had been. Statements that had previously seemed egregious mistakes, now seemed at worst near misses within a powerful and generally successful tradition. That sort of experience—the pieces suddenly sorting themselves out and coming together in a new way—is the first general characteristic of revolutionary change.[8]

Note Kuhn's exact choice of words in describing his flash of insight. We see the "fragments in my head sorted themselves out in a new way" and "the pieces suddenly sorting themselves out and coming together in a new way." The recombination is spontaneous, not a product of Kuhn's own will. Quite the opposite. He was working on a very different problem: why Aristotle was wrong. Instead he solved the problem of how Aristotle was right. All of the pieces came from Aristotle's own work. Kuhn invented none of the elements. He—or rather his brain acting on its own—just brought them together in a new way.

Note that he "gazed abstractedly out the window." For a moment he stopped thinking about the problem he was working on. He paused. For a moment he was not really thinking at all.

Only then could his brain bring together the new combination. Kuhn explains in *Structure* that scientists do not know beforehand what problem they will solve. The problem and solution arise at the same time.

Once Kuhn understood that Aristotle was right—as he always knew that Newton was right—he understood how Copernicus could link the two. A change in paradigm does not mean that bad ideas give way to good ones. Instead, one good idea gives way to another. Aristotle and Ptolemy after him solved many key scientific problems of their age. Copernicus and then Newton solved other problems. Einstein went on to solve different problems still. Ptolemy was just as good a scientist as Copernicus: the Ptolemy star maps served as the basis for maritime navigation right up to the late 1990s, when satellites and computer models—as GPS— finally put them to pasture. And engineers around the world use Newton's physics, not Einstein's, for everything they build.

Good ideas replacing good ideas—and sometimes coexisting— mean that scientists never prove anything. Instead they offer evidence that supports the solution to a particular problem. After Einstein, quantum physics went on to show that no scientific measurement is ever 100 percent accurate, so there is no such thing as an accurate prediction—the famous Heisenberg uncertainty principle:

> In the strict formulation of the causal law—if we know the present, we can calculate the future—it is not the conclusion that is wrong, but the premise.[9]

Scientists are always positing approximations of the truth, some closer than others, but all subject to revision as further evidence arises. You accept theories and methods—and combinations thereof—according to how well they work for the problems that interest you and your field at the time. In this way science is "pragmatic," as William James would call it. In *Pragmatism: A New Name for Some Old Ways of Thinking* (1907), James gave the field of philosophy its first major American contribution, though he frankly admits that it's hardly new. He wrote:

> Any idea upon which we can ride . . . any idea that will carry us prosperously from one part of our experience to any other part . . . is true for just so much, true in so far forth, true instrumentally. . . . This is the "instrumental" view of truth . . . the view that truth in our ideas means their power to "work."[10]

To James, pragmatism is not anti-theory. On the contrary, it welcomes all theories:

> As the young Italian pragmatist Papini has well said, it lies in the midst of our theories, like a corridor in a hotel. Innumerable chambers open out of it. In one you may find a man writing an atheistic volume; in the next some one on his knees praying for faith and strength; in a third a chemist investigating a body's properties. In a fourth a system of idealistic metaphysics is being ex-cogitated; in a fifth the impossibility of metaphysics is being shown. But they all own the corridor, and all must pass through it if they want a practicable way of getting in or out of their respective rooms.[11]

For James, a theory gets out of its "room" to do something useful in the real world. For that, it must become pragmatic to some degree, or rather whoever uses the theory must do so. You find a fit between one or more theories and a situation where they are useful in that combination. But not all situations have a solution, even a pragmatic one. Achievement follows the possibilities that previous elements allow, not the will of the scientist. Does this mean you should not work hard on a problem, because the flash of insight will solve a different problem? Not at all. You have to understand the original problem thoroughly for your mind to touch on all the pieces you need for the answer. It's just that you need to open your mind to other pieces from other problems, because those will combine for a new solution to a new problem. And that new problem is often quite close to the one you were working on.

That flashes of insight solve problems different to some degree from what the scientist intended has major implications for other forms of human endeavor. It goes against common wisdom on how great achievements happen, where first you set your goal, then you work hard to achieve it. That's not how it really works: the achievement and goal arise at the same time. In later chapters we will find this same pattern in other fields of human endeavor, where flashes of insight make unpredictable new combinations from previous elements. Our examples include the computer revolution, civil rights in the United States, and many other familiar examples that we view in a new light, the way Kuhn did with famous scientific advances.

The combination of previous elements in a flash of insight is the essence of strategic intuition. It plays a key role in the first part of the scientific method, where you study the work of other scientists to come up with a hypothesis worth testing. In science, the result of strategic intuition is a strategy, that is, a course of action toward a goal: an experiment to test your new hypothesis. In other fields the result is the same: a flash of insight gives you a goal and a course of action to reach it. Your goal is a hypothesis: you think it will work, but only the experiment—the course of action—will tell you for sure.

That's why strategic intuition is strategic: the flash of insight gives you a strategy. For all kinds of achievement, it guides what strategy you take. Thanks to Kuhn, we see that strategic intuition is also scientific. We can now identify two major steps in the scientific method: strategic intuition to give you an idea and the experimental method to test it. The rest of this book reveals further how that first step works in other fields of endeavor.

3

Two Halves of a Brain

Intelligent Memory in Neuroscience

How does a flash of insight give you an idea for action? For a long time scientists believed that this flash of insight came from the right hemisphere of the brain, where creative, imaginative, and intuitive thoughts occur. The left hemisphere of the brain handles logical, analytical, and rational thoughts. In 1981 Roger Sperry won the Nobel Prize for his research on the two-sided brain. In his Nobel lecture, he noted the following:

> The same individual can be observed to employ consistently one or the other of two distinct forms of mental approach and strategy, much like two different people, depending on whether the left or right hemisphere is in use.[1]

From the 1960s through the 1990s, the two-sided brain became a common explanation for the existence of two kinds of people, two kinds of thinking, and even two kinds of organizations. You might say "I'm a left-brain person" or "Use your right brain on this" or "We're a left-brain company." Debate arose over whether women were right-brained and men left-brained. Brain scans showed that Japanese use the right hemisphere of their brains more. Was this the reason why their economy slowed down in the 1990s?

Yet in Kuhn's description of scientific achievement, a flash of insight seems to combine both sides of the brain: a creative flash yields a rational insight. The pieces of Aristotle's physics came together in Kuhn's mind as a logical whole in a stroke of intuition. For Copernicus, Aristarchus plus trigonometry plus Ptolemaic data were rational elements that came together as a rational hypothesis to test. The elements and the result are rational; the means of combination are intuitive. Does this mean the creative right side of the brain reaches across to the analytical left side for elements to combine and then moves the result to the left side of the brain? Sperry said that each side works independently: the creative side cannot draw from the analytical side. If so, flashes of insight lack content: how can you put together a puzzle with no pieces to work with?

As it turns out, in the late 1990s neuroscience overturned Sperry's model. Eric Kandel won the Nobel Prize in 2000 for his research on a new model of how the brain works. Today, scientists no longer believe that one side of the brain is creative and the other side rational. The new model puts intuition and analysis together in all modes of thought. There is no such thing as "pure analysis" or "pure intuition." All your thoughts are flashes of insight to some degree. You may not notice the small ones. The big ones change your strategy. This new model of the brain explains how strategic intuition can be logical and creative at the same time.

To understand the new model of the brain and how it differs from Sperry's, let's go back and see how Sperry came up with his model in the first place. He was a very good scientist. How could he be so wrong? As Kuhn saw for Aristotle, perhaps Sperry was right about something, and the new model is simply more right about more things. Let's see what Sperry was right about, and wrong about, and why.

Sperry's work began during World War II—almost four centuries after Copernicus'. Sperry's first research subject was an American soldier, known in the study as W.J.—a high-school graduate of above-average intelligence, who liked to read Greek history and the novels of Victor Hugo.[2] In September 1944, W.J. was part of the largest airborne assault in history, when thousands of paratroopers landed in Holland. Something went wrong with W.J.'s parachute. He survived the fall, with a broken leg and a blow to the head that knocked him out for two days. The Germans captured him, and a guard knocked him out again with a rifle butt to the skull.

The war ended a few months later, and W.J. went home to Los Angeles. His leg healed, but he never fully recovered from those two blows to the head. He began to lose his sense of time. One morning he drove off and found himself fifty miles away that afternoon with no idea of what happened in the hours between. In 1951, after an operation on his intestines, he suffered an epileptic fit. From then on seizures came often and grew worse. By 1956 he was averaging two to three seizures a day. His seizures were preceded by a dizzy sensation, like a Ferris wheel spinning, and then his head would involuntarily turn to the left. He fell to the ground in violent convulsions that sometimes knocked him unconscious.

By 1962 W.J. averaged up to ten seizures a day and suffered cuts and bruises from his many falls. Once he even fell into a fire. His doctors tried all combinations of drugs, but nothing worked. The seizures were ruining his life. At that point J. E. Bogen and P. J. Vogel, two doctors at the Loma Linda School of Medicine, proposed a new kind of surgery. They would cut his brain in half.

The procedure was called a callosotomy. The two halves of the brain are connected by a white cord of nerves, the corpus callosum ("callus body" in Latin), which looks like a long, thick callus. Some 200 million nerves make up the corpus callosum—more than all the nerves that connect the brain to the rest of the body. Injuries to different sides of the brain have different effects: loss of speech or memory or movement in various limbs. Scientists believed that the brain coordinated these functions by sending electrical signals through the corpus callosum, allowing a person, for example, to look at a pencil and reach for it at the same time.[3]

The corpus callosum played a role in epilepsy, or so many doctors thought. A fit of epilepsy starts small on one side of the brain, spreads to the other side, and then becomes a full-blown seizure. Cut the cord between the two sides, and you stop the seizures— perhaps. During World War II two doctors at the University of Rochester performed partial callosotomies on twenty-four epilep- tic patients, but with mixed results. At Loma Linda, Bogen and Vogel went over the Rochester reports and decided to try again, this time by cutting the cord completely. On February 4, 1962, they severed W.J.'s corpus callosum.

When W.J. woke up, he was able to hear, open his eyes, move his toes, stick out his tongue, and grasp with his right hand. But he could not speak, feed himself, or move any other part of his body. This condition lasted a week. Slowly he regained movement in his body. Many times a day a seizure would start on the right side of his brain but would die out before it gained any force. When he got stronger the doctors gave him drugs again. The sei- zures stopped completely, and W.J. gained forty pounds. He and his family slept through the night for the first time in more than a decade.

After six months W.J.'s doctors declared him cured. Callosoto- mies became a standard procedure to cure severe epilepsy when drugs fail to work. Today in the United States more than a hun- dred callosotomy procedures are performed every year.

W.J.'s operation earned him a place in the history of epilepsy. But that was not all. Bogen invited Roger Sperry, a scientist from the California Institute of Technology, to conduct psychology tests on W.J. after the surgery. Bogen knew about Sperry's work from a 1961 article in *Science* magazine, where Sperry reported how he cut live animal brains in half and then tested the animals' behav- ior. Sperry concluded: "The split brain behaves in many respects like two separate brains."[4] Now, thanks to Bogen, Sperry had a human subject to work with next.

Sperry gave W.J. his animal tests and added others that pro- vided much more information, because unlike animals W.J. could follow instructions and answer Sperry's questions. These tests all set out to stimulate one side of the brain and observe whether the other side responds. Which stimuli work on one side of the brain and not the other side tell us what each side of the brain can do. Sperry blindfolded W.J. and placed something in his right hand: a pencil, cigarette, ring, pistol, hat, glasses, and other such everyday objects. Sperry asked him to use the object and then name and describe it in words. When W.J. used his right hand, he could use each object and name it too. When he used his left hand, he could use each object but could neither name nor describe it.

Sperry's research assistant, Michael Gazzaniga, reported:

Nothing can possibly replace a singular memory of mine: that of the moment when I discovered that case W.J. could no longer verbally describe (from his left hemisphere) stimuli presented to his freshly disconnected right hemisphere. An experiment I had designed, executed and carried out alone as a mere graduate student at Caltech had worked. With it, the modern split-brain story was born.[5]

Here Gazzaniga rightly claimed some glory for himself and also gave us the precise moment the Sperry team knew they were on the right track. The tests showed that the right brain does not process language, but that it does handle complex tasks. The left brain does both. The left brain might be smarter than the right, but the right brain was not completely entirely dumb.

After fourteen weeks of experiments, W.J. left the scene and went on with his life. Sperry went on to perform finer experiments with Bogen and Vogel's other split-brain patients, teasing out more precisely the nature of intelligence in the two sides of the brain.

The next breakthrough came in 1968 when Sperry and Jerre Levy-Agresti designed a new kind of experiment:

Tests were performed in which three-dimensional forms held in the right or left hand had to be matched with their unfolded shapes drawn as expanded patterns on cards and presented visually.

It was found that the right, minor hemisphere was much superior to the left. Further, the mechanisms used by the two hemispheres in solving the problems appeared to be different, as indicated by the nature of the problems that proved to be easy or difficult. The data indicate that the mute, minor hemisphere is specialized for Gestalt perception, being primarily a synthesist in dealing with information input. The speaking, major hemisphere, in contrast, seems to operate in a more logical, analytic computer-like fashion. Its language is inadequate for the rapid complex syntheses achieved by the minor hemisphere.[6]

These "rapid complex syntheses" of "Gestalt perception" are flashes of insight. Sperry and Levy-Agresti claimed to have found where they happen: in the right side of the brain. For the first time we see the "minor" side of the brain—the right—do a complex task better than the "major" left side. Maybe the left side was not smarter than the right. Maybe they were equally smart but in two different ways. For the first time in history Sperry and Levy-Agresti produced solid scientific evidence of two successful modes of thought: quick and synthetic flashes of insight on one side of the brain and slow and logical analysis on the other.

Sperry gave Levy-Agresti equal credit for this joint breakthrough in his Nobel lecture. His prize in the field of physiology and medicine was the first in the field of psychology research. Sperry went on to also win awards in psychology and philosophy. When he died in 1994 many scientists agreed with Sperry that the right side of the brain was not only equal but superior to the left: the left brain helps you do the analytical things, but the intuitive right side gives you the creative edge to innovate and succeed in the fast-changing modern world.

Or does it?

Sperry himself was not so sure, as he noted in his Nobel lecture:

In some cases the conclusions along with the growing wave of semi-popular extrapolations and speculations concerning "left-brain" vs. "right-brain" functions call for a word of caution. The left–right dichotomy in cognitive mode is an idea with which it is very easy to run wild. Qualitative shifts in mental control may involve up–down, front–back, or various other organizational changes as well as left–right differences. Furthermore, in the normal state the two hemispheres appear to work closely together as a unit, rather than one being turned on while the other idles. Much yet remains to be settled in all these matters. Even the main idea of differential left and right cognitive modes is still under challenge in some quarters.[7]

Above all, Sperry was a good scientist. He believed in what he said, but he also knew he might be wrong. Contradictory evidence had already begun to appear, thanks to new medical techniques beyond the callosotomy. Early versions of computerized axial tomography (CAT) scans and magnetic resonance imaging (MRI) gave scientists a new window into the workings of the human brain without cutting it in half. Two CAT pioneers, Allan McLeod Hounsfield and Godfrey Newbold Cormack, won the Nobel Prize in 1979, two years, in fact, before Sperry did.

In 1990 Seiji Ogawa at Bell Laboratories in New Jersey figured out how to keep the MRI on while the brain was working. Instead of one snapshot, like an X-ray, it was possible to make a series of images similar to a cartoon strip that showed the brain in action. In 1993, in the last months of Sperry's life, Ogawa made a further advance that showed the human brain's higher cognitive functions. Ogawa's first MRIs were crude and shadowy, filled with more dark than light. But they clearly show both sides of the brain working at the same time.[8]

Sperry's suspicions were right. It's not just left versus right but also up versus down, front versus back, deep versus shallow, gray matter versus white matter, folds versus smooth—it seemed as if a single thought sparked activity in different brain areas on both the left and the right sides. Following Ogawa, scientists quickly developed ever more detailed maps of the brain. The left–right distinction faded away. The brain was like a big mosaic, with no obvious pattern of any kind.

As Kuhn says, a major advance does not mean the previous paradigm was wrong. The MRI advances did not cancel out Sperry's achievement. He was right about one important point: different areas of the brain do different things. But now we know that there are dozens, hundreds, maybe thousands of different areas—not just left and right. Most important, Sperry drew scientists' attention to the nonlogical functions of the brain as a missing link in research for how the mind works. Sperry tried to find out where creativity, imagination, and intuition happen in the brain. If they don't happen in the right brain, as Sperry thought, then how does the new model of the brain explain them?

Research on split-brain patients shows how the brain makes adjustments when the left and right sides can't communicate. But MRIs of normal brains—with the corpus callosum intact—show both sides of the brain firing. For complex tasks the split brain fires on one side. Normal brains fire on both sides. The right side of the brain is not the location of creativity, intuition, and imagination: the new mosaic model of the brain shows how these functions spread out to a different set of locations for every different task. The same is true for logical, analytical, and rational tasks. The mosaic model takes the old left–right functions and scatters them in multiple pieces throughout the brain.[9]

As it turns out, research on another epileptic patient, H.M., helped provide the basis for the new mosaic model. H.M. underwent a different treatment for his seizures—surgeons removed part of his lower brain, including the hippocampus. This led Brenda Milner of McGill University to discover the key role of the hippocampus in how the brain works.[10] Hippocampus means "seahorse" in Greek, and that's what it looks like. You have two hippocampuses: one on the right side and one on the left. They curl around just under your ear, deep inside the brain. In 2000 Eric Kandel of Columbia University won the Nobel Prize for showing the chemical and physical changes behind what Milner observed in H.M. In his Nobel lecture, Kandel gave Milner due credit and cited dozens of other scientists who contributed to the new model of the brain.[11]

The mosaic memory model carries forward Sperry's achievements on brain geography and intuitive thought but shows these elements in a very different light. The new paradigm is so new that there is no one name for it yet. Here we will use the most common name to date: intelligent memory. The neuroscientist Barry Gordon used that as a title for his 2003 book on the subject, where he says:

> Intelligent Memory . . . is like connecting dots to form a picture. The dots are pieces or ideas, the lines between them are your connections or associations. The lines can coalesce into larger fragments, and these fragments can merge to form a whole thought. This whole thought may be a visual image, a piece of knowledge, an idea, or even a solution to a problem. Individual pieces, the connections, and the mental processing that orchestrates them generally work together so they appear to be a single cognitive event. That's what happens when ideas or concepts "pop" into your mind.[12]

Here we see flashes of insight as a normal function of the brain: something pops into your mind. When a few fragments merge easily to form a simple thought, you don't even notice the pop. When more fragments take a longer time to merge, to form a complex thought, you notice it. The fragments are memories. Old ones form by the hippocampus firing to etch them wherever the brain might put them. New memories are simply whatever you took in a moment ago. Old and new memories make up the fragments that flashes of insight merge into thoughts.

Intelligent memory makes your brain the greatest inventory system on earth. Through your life you take in information all the time through your five senses. The brain takes the information apart—neuroscientists call that parsing—and stores the pieces on different shelves. A series of nerve impulses then carry the pieces of information to various storage locations and then stimulate other nerves to store them. The next piece of information fires up a different set of transit nerves and a different set of storage nerves. The brain remembers each intake, parsing, travel, and arrival at storage as a unique event. The trail of nerves lit up leaves an afterglow. That glow is short-term memory.

Short-term memory becomes stronger in four ways: repetition, attention, surprise, and association. For example, if you notice that the person above the nametag looks like your sister, that's association. A stronger short-term memory lights up the hippocampus, which keeps the short-term memory lit up for a much longer time, and this in turn stimulates the storage nerves to grow bigger or to spread the charge to neighboring nerves. That makes more space on the shelf for this one memory.

A short-term memory can create a temporary pattern in your frontal lobes, the front of your brain behind your forehead. Scientists call that *working memory*. When you think, you pull existing short-term memories into the front of your brain, and from there these memories connect to related long-term memories. A subset of the two kinds of memories come together (binding, the opposite of parsing) as a flash of insight large or small. The result is a thought.[13]

Intelligent memory unites reason, logic, and analysis with creativity, intuition, and imagination as a single mode of thought. Sperry described analysis and intuition as "inbuilt, qualitatively different and mutually antagonistic modes of cognitive processing"—like oil and water, they cannot mix. In contrast, intelligent memory puts them together as elements of the same thought. You can have more or less of one or the other, but every thought needs both. All rational thinking require automatic storage, retrieval, and combination. The last step—automatic combination—is intuition. It works in all kinds of thought. It is not a mode of thought by itself.

In later chapters we will examine more closely how flashes of insight combine analysis and intuition and we will note the implications of this combination for human achievements of various kinds. Intelligent memory reveals the biological mechanism of how strategic intuition works, where past elements stored in memory combine in a flash of insight to give you an idea for action.[14] Sperry believed that intuition made life creative, and he made it equal to analysis by giving it half the brain. But intelligent memory goes one step further: it makes intuition the creative part of all kinds of thought, including analysis. Strategic intuition projects intelligent memory into the future, as a course of action to follow, based solidly on the past.

4

Lieutenant M Saves Your Life

Expert Intuition in Action

This chapter takes intelligent memory out of the neuroscience lab and into real life. In the laboratory you give your subjects one task at a time and study how they do it. In real life you decide not only how to do a task but also which task to do. Does intelligent memory work for both? Deciding which task to do means setting a goal, and deciding how to do it means choosing a course of action. The result is a strategy. In intelligent memory this strategy comes from a flash of insight that brings past elements together in your brain. In a laboratory, magnetic resonance imaging (MRI) can reveal small flashes you don't even feel. But larger ones, like Kuhn's epiphany about Aristotle, don't happen in a laboratory. We have no way to re-create in a laboratory the unforeseen moment Kuhn gazed out the window and saw the flash.

But a research psychologist, Gary Klein, does the next best thing. He follows experts into action—soldiers, firefighters, and emergency room nurses—and asks them afterward how they decided to do what they did. Klein pioneered the empirical study of expert intuition: how intelligent memory brings elements from past experiences to bear upon similar situations. These are flashes of insight smaller than strategic intuition, but in essence they work the same way in the brain. If you've seen or done something many times, the brain can pull the relevant memories off the shelf quickly. That's expert intuition at work. In strategic intuition the brain also draws on elements that come from beyond your own experience, the way Copernicus drew on Aristarchus.

Expert intuition works fast, in familiar situations. Strategic intuition works more slowly, in new situations. But the basic mechanism is the same. Expert intuition is easier to study because you know when the expert will probably use it. In strategic intuition flashes of insight happen at any time of any day. In expert intuition they happen whenever the expert swings into action. That's what Klein set out to study: what exactly goes on in the minds of experts in action. He gives us an in-depth look at how intelligent memory works in real life. We will see what Klein tells us about how expert intuition works and then ask how that applies to strategic intuition.

Klein started out as a laboratory researcher at the University of Pittsburgh. In the summer of 1985 he left the laboratory to study his first set of subjects in action: firefighters in Cleveland. In the laboratory you give subjects a goal and several options to reach it, in order to see how they weigh the options and make a decision. But firefighters don't have time for that. They have to act quickly. Instead, Klein recalls, "I expected that they would only come up with two leading options, and compare those to each other."[1]

His chance to test this hypothesis came on his first afternoon in the firehouse. The alarm rang but not for a fire. It was a serious injury. The emergency rescue team swung into action, with Lieutenant M in charge. Klein rode along to the scene. Later he interviewed the lieutenant to learn exactly how he made his decisions. Here's what happened:

> The rescue truck speeds through town. It jerks to a stop on a suburban street. People hurry toward a man lying in a pool of blood next to a house. A woman crouches over him. As Lieutenant M runs to the man, he makes his diagnosis: the amount of blood means a cut artery. The man's wife holds dishcloths over the wound, and the shape and location of the stains on the cloth tell Lieutenant M which artery exactly. He falls to his knees by the man's side and applies firm pressure to just the right spot. The woman quickly explains that her husband slipped on a ladder and his hand went

through a pane of glass. Protocol tells Lieutenant M to look for other wounds that might prevent him from moving the victim, but he never even considers that. He sees there is too much blood lost already. They have to move him right away no matter what else might be wrong. They should put the victim into inflatable pants to raise his blood pressure, but Lieutenant M skips that as well, to save more time. He assigns his strongest but newest crew member to bear the greatest weight of the stretcher, trading speed for the risk of dropping it. They get the stretcher in without harm. In the back of the rescue truck, speeding to the hospital, the crew puts on the inflatable pants. They reach the hospital exactly ten minutes after the bell rang in the firehouse. The hospital crew takes over. The rescue is a complete success.[2]

In the interview Lieutenant M reported to Klein that each decision he made came as a single idea. Never once did he set a goal, list options, weigh the options, and decide among them. First he applied pressure, then he picked the strongest but newest crew member to bear the greatest weight of the stretcher, and then in the truck they put the victim into the inflatable pants. Formal protocol or normal procedure certainly gave him other options— examine the victim for other wounds before moving him, put the victim into the inflatable pants right away, and assign someone experienced to bear the greatest weight of the stretcher—but Lieutenant M never considered them. His actions came from a single option arising in his mind, and then the next one, and then the next one, on through the whole event.

Klein went on to study more firefighters responding to more calls and found the same thing: "I was wrong. The firefighters, especially the more experienced ones, some with over twenty years of experience, usually just considered a single option. . . . This was a finding I hadn't expected. I had stumbled onto the phenomenon of intuition."[3] Klein's discovery came as a flash of insight to a new paradigm of how decision making really happens. The age-old analytical model—list options, weigh them, and decide which is best—was wrong. Klein and his followers went on to study more firefighters, then soldiers in battle, then emergency room nurses, and eventually members of many other professions. Every time, they found the same phenomenon that Klein observed when Lieutenant M saved a man's life. As Klein later wrote: "Our research led us to the conclusion that we are all intuitive decision makers. Some of us are more skilled than others, certainly, and some are more specialized, but all of us rely on intuition."[4]

Klein discovered how flashes of insight from intelligent memory work in real life as people decide what to do. Lieutenant M's brain took in pieces of information as short-term memory. He drew some of that into his working memory, where it mixed with selected bits of his long-term memory. He could remember the color of the house—it was in his short-term memory—but that did not make it into his working memory, as the color of the house didn't matter. The amount of blood was another story. In his working memory that short-term memory mixed with his long-term memory from training or previous experience. Together they showed him a single course of action—apply pressure, skip the examination and the inflatable pants, and get the strong one to bear the greatest weight of the stretcher. Elements came together in his mind, in sequence, as flashes of insight that told him what to do.

Klein now specializes in studying experts who act quickly and have enough education to explain later what went through their minds as they acted. Klein tells us, "I never set out to study intuition."[5] But as with all major flashes of insight, his discovery changed his goal. In later chapters we will see how intelligent memory applies to unfamiliar situations too—as strategic intuition—but here we want to see how widely Klein's expert intuition applies. Are there any fields of human endeavor beyond the reach of expert intuition?

We immediately wonder about fields where decision making happens more slowly, especially highly analytical fields that use a lot of numbers. Does expert intuition apply to them? On the slow front Klein had a distinguished predecessor in Herbert Simon, who won the Nobel Prize for Economics in 1978. Simon offered an alternative to the prevailing theory of rational "economic man" who maximizes utility under perfect information. On the contrary, what people really do is search for a course of action that's good enough. Simon used laboratory research but with experts who suit that locale: chess players. They sit in a room making decisions, as in other laboratory experiments. But instead of tasks the researchers make up, chess players engage in their expert activity: playing chess. The chess players make decisions much more slowly than Lieutenant M saving a life, so Simon could study them closely.[6]

Simon found that expert chess players do consider multiple options, but in sequence, not all together. They think through the first option that strikes them as promising. In thinking it through they might see a major flaw and give it up. Or it suffices and they go ahead and do it. If they give it up, they think through the next option that strikes them as promising. And so on through the game. They don't compare several options against each other. And where does each option come from? They recognize elements from previous games they have seen or played. Simon explained:

In particular, recognition of familiar patterns is a major component of expert skill, and experts can consequently replace a great deal of heuristic search with solutions, or partial solutions, that they discover by recognition. Moreover, problem solving by recognition has all the characteristics of what is usually called "intuitive," "judgmental," or even "creative" problem solving. . . . The experimental data show that masters and grandmasters search very selectively, using their recognition of cues to guide the selectivity. They search the right part of the space of possible move sequences, achieving great computational efficiency.[7]

Simon went on to find the same results with physicists solving problems in a classroom setting.[8] Note that for Simon, creative problem solving yields great computational efficiency. Simon, Klein, and the science of intelligent memory erase the line between creative and intuitive thinking on the one hand and rational and analytical thinking on the other: decision making combines both, as flashes of insight that show the answer.

But aren't there any analytical tasks without the intuitive elements of recognition and combination? For example, consider the sum below. Is it correct?

$$
\begin{array}{r}
28 \\
+32 \\
\hline
60
\end{array}
$$

To solve this problem you use pure analysis, logic, and reason—right? If so, try this one.

$$
\begin{array}{r}
\kappa\eta \\
+ \,\lambda\beta \\
\hline
\xi\varsigma
\end{array}
$$

Did you feel your brain search? It looked on the shelves of your memory to find these symbols. Chances are, your brain did not find these symbols. This is the same sum (28 + 32 = 60) but in ancient Greek. Both versions are correct, but you need far more than analysis, logic, and reason to get the answer. In the version you recognize the numbers and their computation came off the shelves of your brain so quickly and smoothly that you did not even realize it happened. But for you to recall them, you must have learned the symbols and their computation sometime before in your life. If by chance you knew ancient Greek, you would recognize the figures in the second sum as well.

Expert intuition starts in infancy. From the moment you open your eyes, move your arms, and hear and smell and taste, your brain parses information and stores it. The hippocampus turns some of the information into long-term memory. You gain expertise in everyday tasks—for example, dressing yourself, brushing your teeth—in the same way you gain expertise in professional tasks later in life. Expert intuition provides the structure of human achievement at its most basic: how you master the tasks you need for success in whatever world you're born to.

Here's another example of expert intuition in mathematics. On the next page, there's another column of numbers with a total at the bottom. Don't look at it yet. Let me give you the instructions first.

Like the first example above, this example has a column made up of positive numbers. Below them is a line and below that a sum. I want you to answer if the sum is right or wrong. Thumb up is right. Thumb down is wrong. When you turn the page, look for only an instant, a single glance, and answer if it's right or wrong: thumb up or thumb down.

Go ahead now. Turn the page and glance at the sum.

If you need to glance again, go ahead. Don't look for any longer than the first time. If you need to do it a third or fourth time, that's fine too.

Did you see it? Did you feel the flash of insight?

The answer is thumb down: the sum is incorrect. It usually takes two or three times to see the answer. The first time you look, your eye goes to the top of the column of numbers, because that's how you learned to do sums. Your brain notices that the column is too long to compute the total in the short moment you see it. The next time or the third time or the fourth time, your eye goes to the bottom instead. A flash of insight matches the size of this number with past sums you have done where the total was just too small for all those numbers above it.

Children in third or fourth grade cannot do this. They have to total the numbers to get the answer. They do not yet have enough sums on the shelves of their brain to know the total is just too small.

This kind of computational shortcut is a key feature of expert intuition in all sorts of mathematical tasks. It's the same as Lieutenant M looking at the shape of the bloodstain on the

Thumb Up or Down?
49
93
22
18
75
30
+87
54

dishcloths over the victim's arm and deciding to skip a detailed examination of the wound. If you're good at analytical tasks, you make this kind of shortcut decision routinely. Expertise works the same way regardless of the task.

Let's look at two recent experiments on intelligent memory for mathematics. These experiments show that analytical tasks not only include intuitive elements but also go better when you turn your mind off the task itself. Relax. Let the brain work out its own connections.

In 2003, in Lübeck, Germany, five scientists—Wagner, Gals, Haider, Verleger, and Born—tested the effect of sleep on solving mathematical problems.[9] They divided a hundred subjects into five groups. The first three groups got training in a similar kind of mathematical problem: to convert a string of eight digits to a different number, following two simple rules the scientists taught them. Training in the rules included three sets of actual problems. After the training came a break of eight hours, of three kinds. Two of these three groups had training in the evening. Later, one of these two groups went to sleep for the night, while the other group stayed awake all night. The third group had its training in the morning and then stayed awake all day.

After the break each of the three groups got ten sets of problems to solve. The problems had a pattern, and once you saw the pattern you could solve the problems quickly. This enabled the scientists to measure whether and when a subject saw the pattern. Thirteen in the sleep group, five in the day group, and five in the sleepless-night group saw the pattern.

The scientists concluded that the pattern came together in the brains of the sleep group during sleep. To confirm that seeing the pattern came from the training and not just from better rest, they administered the problems to a fourth group that had a full night's sleep and to a fifth group at the end of a normal day. Neither group saw the pattern. The scientists concluded that the elements of the solution went into the sleep group's brains during training and that during sleep the elements came together in a new combination.

The Lübeck scientists point out that the sleep group went to sleep not knowing there was a pattern to identify. Both the problem and its solution came together in the minds of the sleep group during sleep. Likewise, as Lieutenant M hopped off the rescue truck he did not yet know what problem he would try to solve. When he saw the shape of the bloodstain and the amount of blood, a goal—getting the victim to the hospital, quickly and alive—and the elements of action—applying pressure on the artery, strongest crew member bearing the greatest weight of the stretcher, and putting the victim into the inflatable pants—arose at the same time.

Klein notes this pattern among experts in general. They do not set a goal first and then plan activities to reach the goal. Instead, the actions and goal come together:

What triggers active problem-solving is the ability to recognize when a goal is reachable. . . . There must be an experiential ability to judge the solvability of problems prior to working on them. Experience lets us recognize the existence of opportunities. When the opportunity is recognized, the problem solver working out its implications is looking for a way to make good use of it, trying to shape it into a reasonable goal.[10]

We will return to the order of goal setting in later chapters where we see how flashes of insight in strategic intuition overturn the conventional notion that goal setting comes first.

Our second experiment of insight in mathematics comes from Amsterdam, Holland. In 2005 four scientists—Dijksterhuis, Bos, Nordgren, and van Baren—asked eighty students to rate different models of cars.[11] For half the cars the scientists gave the students twelve attributes to consider—such as price, miles per gallon, and age. For the other half they gave the students four attributes. All the students read the information about the cars. After that the scientists asked half the students to think about the information for four minutes. They distracted the other half with anagrams to solve, also for four minutes. When the four minutes were up, they asked all the students to rate the cars.

For the simple computation—with four attributes—nearly 60 percent of the *thinking* students picked the best car, compared with just over 40 percent of the *distracted* students. For the complex computation—with twelve attributes—just over 20 percent of the thinking students picked the best car, compared with 60 percent of the distracted students. The scientists concluded that the thinking students did a bit better on the simple computation, while the distracted students did much better on the complex one. All the students took in the same information, but the brain of the distracted student found the right combination far better than the brain of the student who spent the same time thinking about the problem.

In both the Lübeck and Amsterdam studies the subjects took in detailed information first, and then their relaxed brains combined it. They did not pull the answer out of thin air. Insight comes from creative combination of real elements on the shelves of your brain. Those elements include mathematical formulas and data. These recent experiments give further support for intelligent memory as a single mode of thought that includes both analysis and intuition. The analysis part was active thinking about the information the subjects took in. The intuition part was the automatic combination of elements to arrive at an answer. In both studies the forced break from analysis helped the scientists identify when intuition took over.

Let's take a final look at the left–right model of the brain, as psychologists tried to explain it in the years after Sperry's Nobel Prize. As Ptolemy's followers adorned the planets with more and more intricate circles to fit them within the circular motion of the other heavenly bodies, psychologists went to great lengths to explain the difference between the two modes of thought. In recent years you see less of that, as intelligent memory spreads from the medical laboratory to the psychology laboratory. For example, the Lübeck sleep study featured psychologists and neuroscientists working together. This kind of collaboration is becoming more common around the world.

But a close look at the old paradigm still helps illuminate the new one. Table 4.1 shows an attempt from 1996 by a psychologist, Steven Sloman of Brown University, to pin down the differences between the two modes of thought. Sloman's recent work tends more toward a single mode of thought,[12] but this table stands out as perhaps the most sophisticated statement on the left–right paradigm before intelligent memory worked its way from neuroscience to psychology.

The first thing we notice from the table is that like Sperry, Sloman elevates intuition—or "associative" reasoning—to equal footing with its rational opposite. Sloman even calls both of them "reasoning," which itself is a promotion for intuition. It's reasonable, not irrational. But is intuition a separate "system," as Sloman calls it? In intelligent memory intuition and analysis are both elements in the overall mosaic memory system. Neither is a system on its own.

Let's look at each row of the table. There are two entries: "associative system" and "rule-based system." Our new understanding of intelligent memory makes us ask the question: Can the brain do one side of the row without doing the other side?

Let's take the first row: similarity and congruity on the intuitive side and symbol manipulation on the rational side. The most

Table 4.1 Characterization of Two Forms of Reasoning

Characteristics	Associative system	Rule-based system
Principles of operation	Similarity and contiguity	Symbol manipulation
Source of knowledge	Personal experience	Language, culture, and formal systems
Nature of representation		
Basic units	Concrete and generic concepts, images, stereotypes, and feature sets	Concrete, generic, and abstract concepts; abstracted features; compositional symbols
Relations	(a) Associations	(a) Causal, logical, and hierarchical
	(b) Soft constraints	(b) Hard constraints
Nature of processing	(a) Reproductive but capable of similarity-based generalization	(a) Productive and systematic
	(b) Overall feature computation and constraint satisfaction	(b) Abstraction of relevant features
	(c) Automatic	(c) Strategic
Illustrative cognitive functions	Intuition	Deliberation
	Fantasy	Explanation
	Creativity	Formal analysis
	Imagination	Verification
	Visual recognition	Ascription of purpose
	Associative memory	Strategic memory

SOURCE: S. Sloman, "The Empirical Case for Two Systems of Reasoning," *Psychological Bulletin* 119, no. 1 (1996): 7. Used with the kind permission of the author.

common symbols we manipulate rationally are letters and numbers. But as we saw in the Greek sum above, you can only manipulate rationally letters and numbers that intuition pulls off the shelves of your brain through similarity and congruity. Without the left side of the row, the right side of the row has nothing to work with. Similarity and congruity—the grease of expert intuition—make symbol manipulation possible.

Let's take the second row: personal experience on the intuitive side and language, culture, and formal systems on the rational side. It is a common mistake to believe that personal experience is only what you do directly. For the human brain personal experience includes what you learn from others, formally through training or informally through watching, listening, and reading. There is no way for the human brain to acquire language, culture, and formal systems except through personal experience. Lieutenant M acquired the language, culture, and formal systems of the firehouse and rescue team by the various experiences of training, watching, or reading or listening to what others did and by his own forays into the field. Once again, both sides of the row work together.

The third row—basic units of representation—seems more or less similar between the two systems. Both have generic and concrete concepts. On one side we also have images, stereotypes, and feature sets. On the other side we have abstract concepts, abstracted features, and compositional symbols. We dealt with symbols in the first row. Abstract concepts and features include images, stereotypes, and feature sets. For example, Lieutenant M's abstract concept of life-threatening injuries comes with images of those injuries from personal experience or learned from others, plus stereotypes that help him group such injuries— bleeding to death from a torn artery—and feature sets that include frantic relatives, the age of the victim, the time it took to get to the scene. Once again it seems like a false exercise to separate the two columns.

Intelligent memory lets us continue through the table, row by row, to show how both sides combine as expert intuition rather than standing apart as two different systems. Perhaps the problem lies in the idea of what a system is. In explaining the table Sloman calls the systems *two forms of computation* and tells how you can program computers using a *rule interpreter* and an *intuitive processor*. This results in two different systems where you can see the different steps and results of each program. In a computer this makes sense. But in the brain you cannot see two different sets of steps and results for the two different systems. There is no hardware or software you can draw a circle around in the brain and call a rule interpreter or intuitive processor. The computer analogy does not work in this case.[13]

The timing of Sloman's table might also help explain why he portrays two modes of thought rather than one. He notes that "[a] psychologically plausible device that can integrate computations from associative networks and symbol-manipulating rules has proven elusive." His table came out only three years after Ogawa's advanced MRIs showed the two sides of the brain working together and two years before Brenda Milner and Eric Kandel made their first full statement on intelligent memory at work.[14] At the time Sloman's table came out we did not have a *plausible device* that integrates the two modes of thought as one. But now, years later, we do.

Let's end our discussion of Sloman's table with a look at the last two rows. Mostly, these rows amount to a restatement of the left–right model of the brain. But note the very last line of each row: *automatic* processing versus *strategic* processing and *associative* memory versus *strategic* memory. This is the most telling distinction of all. No matter how much analytical tasks in the real world depend on expert intuition, there is a difference between doing a task and deciding which task to do. Expert intuition helps you fight a fire, but does it help you decide which fire to fight? Does expert intuition tell you how to organize your firehouse to be ready to fight the right fires or to decide where to put your firehouse in the first place?

Expert intuition makes you better at tactics, but what makes you better at strategy? Expert intuition works for familiar situations, but what about new ones? What good is expert intuition—drawing elements from the past—when the future is unpredictable? If you automatically apply the past to the future, and the future is different, you're making a big mistake. That's where strategy comes in. Expert intuition works for the small picture but not the big one. For the bigger picture we need something else. The old left–right model of the brain gave that task to rational analysis. But if there is no such thing as "rational analysis"—if all thinking combines both sides of Sloman's table—then what do we do about strategy?

As we will see in the following chapters, intelligent memory works in a similar way for strategy as it does for tactics. It's the same mechanism as Lieutenant M and the torn artery, except that elements from a wider variety of sources combine in your mind as a more complex course of action. You do not recognize the whole situation you face as familiar: you recognize parts of it. It's a new situation, but it's made up of pieces that existed before. The future comes from the past, even in scientific revolutions, as Kuhn has made clear. A flash of insight in strategic intuition pulls together disparate pieces of the past to make up your future strategy. From expert intuition to strategic intuition: that's where we go to next.

5

The Corsican Conquers Europe

Coup d'Oeil in Classical Military Strategy

In the history of strategy 1810 stands out as key for two reasons. First, 1810 is the year that the word *strategy* entered the English language. That is very late for an ordinary English word: *tactics*, in contrast, entered English in 1626, nearly two centuries earlier. Second, 1810 is the year that Carl von Clausewitz became a strategist. He was thirty years old at the time, an ambitious Prussian army officer with an intellectual mind. He entered the Berlin War Academy as a student in 1801, the year it was founded, and he graduated three years later at the top of his class. He went on to active duty, fought in a major Prussian defeat, and spent two years as a prisoner. Freed in 1808, he joined a small staff reorganizing the Prussian army. In 1810 he returned to the academy as a professor of strategy. Von Clausewitz went on to become the leading theorist on strategy in the Western world and remains so to this day.

It was no coincidence that strategy entered the English language and von Clausewitz became a scholar of strategy at the same time. The year 1810 was the height of Napoleon Bonaparte's military success. In his time Napoleon ranked as the most successful battlefield general in recorded history. He won battle after battle against larger armies. His victories took him from a modest background in Corsica, with a thick accent that the French elite laughed at, to emperor of Europe in less than a decade. His enemies started studying him, to see how he won, so they could defeat him. And so began the scholarly study of strategy.

Strategy was hardly a new idea. Essays on the subject date back to Sun Tzu's *The Art of War* and Thucydides' *Peloponnesian War*, both from around 400 B.C. But 1810 marks the start of strategy as a formal field of knowledge. In the later nineteenth century strategy spread from military academies to business. Today strategy is a major field of study in management science for all kinds of organizations throughout the world. And the leading classic in the field of strategy remains *On War* by von Clausewitz, first published in 1832.

In explaining Napoleon's success, von Clausewitz singles out one idea as most important. He writes in German, but for this one concept he uses a French term: "coup d'oeil." The word is hard to pronounce for English speakers ("koo-DUY"). We see the word "coup" in it, which we recognize from coup d'état—a strike at the state. Coup d'oeil is a strike of the eye: a glance. Armed with our knowledge of modern neuroscience we can look back on the coup d'oeil of von Clausewitz and see that it is the same basic idea of a flash of insight from intelligent memory. Thomas Kuhn applied it to scientific advance, Gary Klein applied it to experts in action, and von Clausewitz applied it to strategy.

On War is hard to read. Military students joke that General Sherman said "War is hell" but reading *On War* is hell too. Von Clausewitz introduces a host of difficult concepts and proceeds to elaborate on them singly and together in a thicket of long, dense prose in the heavy, academic style of the German Idealists from Kant to Hegel. But one thing is clear: coup d'oeil is the key to strategy. Von Clausewitz writes:

> This facile coup d'oeil of the General, this simple art of forming notions, this personification of the whole action of War, is so entirely and completely the soul of the right method of conducting War, that in no other but this broad way is it possible to conceive that freedom of the mind which is indispensable if it is to dominate events, not be overpowered by them.[1]

Napoleon was known for flashes of insight throughout his life, and Von Clausewitz set out to explain them. In order to understand what von Clausewitz says, let's look at a modern re-creation of Napoleon's coup d'oeil in action. *Napoleon,* by Abel Gance, is one of the great works from the early silent period of cinema: the premiere in 1927 was the first time the Paris Opera showed a film instead of a live performance. In a few short minutes of the film Gance portrays with remarkable economy the role of coup d'oeil in Napoleon's first victory.

The scene takes place during the siege of Toulon in September 1793. Toulon was the French navy's most important port on the southern coast. The British invade and take it. The army of the French Revolution surrounds the city and prepares a counterattack. Napoleon is twenty-four years old at the time. He arrives in Toulon and reports for duty.

The scene begins when Napoleon comes through a doorway and steps inside a spacious country café. He wears a simple black uniform and his famous hat with the crown like an upturned boat—it was standard issue for officers of the day. Under one arm he carries a thick book. He pauses to look around. The café is filled with soldiers in uniform lounging and drinking. There are politicians in fancy dress and dandy hats and all sorts of hangers-on from the countryside. A French general sits at the center of a long table. There is no sign of military discipline. Napoleon strides over to the general. He salutes, hands the general his orders, and stands stiff at attention.

Napoleon's orders post him as second-in-command of the siege artillery. The general looks at the paper and scoffs. They don't need artillery: "We shall take Toulon with the sword and bayonet!" Napoleon gives the hint of a smile, salutes, and turns to go. The general catches his arm and asks, "If you were in my place, little man, what would you do?" Another soldier brings a map and spreads it out on the table before the general.

Napoleon looks down at the map of Toulon for a moment and then looks off into the distance. The filmmaker shows what

Napoleon sees in his mind as a swirl of activity on the map. Then Napoleon blinks, as if coming out of a trance. He places a finger on the map and says, "Once the fort of l'Aiguillette is taken the English will abandon the town."

The general explodes with laughter along with everyone else. But Napoleon just stands still with his face calm. The laughter dies down, and it becomes clear that with a single coup d'oeil Napoleon has won everyone's allegiance away from the general.

This scene is an excellent depiction of Napoleon's coup d'oeil. The general wanted to storm the fortress of Toulon with sword and bayonet, but Napoleon saw a different strategy: take a small fort nearby and the enemy will leave. As it turns out, the general went ahead with his plan. It failed miserably. Paris fired him. The next general listened to Napoleon and took the little fort instead. Napoleon's idea worked. His career took off from there.

The scene in Gance's film is remarkably accurate, except for one thing: we know that Napoleon's coup d'oeil did not take place on command like that, in reply to the general's request. Napoleon put his strategy together over several days and talked with other junior officers about it. Military historians know the elements that Napoleon put together to make his winning idea: contour maps, plus the light cannon, plus the American Revolutionary War, plus Joan of Arc. Let's look at each element to see what part it played in the strategy.

First come contour maps. Napoleon did not invent them—they dated from about a hundred years before—but he was one of the first officers to use them for every battle. On the contour map of Toulon he noticed a small fort, l'Aiguillette, on a cliff overlooking the harbor. Second comes the light cannon. Napoleon did not invent that either—it dated from about ten years before. Unlike the heavy cannon that had defended castles for centuries the new cannon was light enough for animals or humans to roll just about anywhere—even up a cliff.

Contour maps and the light cannon were the tools of Napoleon's trade. He learned how to use them in military school. If contour maps and light cannon were the only elements he put together in his mind, then Napoleon's coup d'oeil would be a simple case of expert intuition in action. There were two more elements that turned Napoleon's coup d'oeil into strategic intuition instead.

The third element of Napoleon's strategy came from the American Revolutionary War. At the siege of Boston Henry Knox had the idea to drag cannons up Dorchester Heights to command the harbor. The British in the town were suddenly afraid of being cut off from their navy. So they got on their ships and sailed away. That was 1776. In 1781 the same thing happened at the siege of Yorktown: the French navy cut off the British troops in town from the British navy at sea. The British surrendered to General George Washington. That ended the war, and from then on the British army was terrified of being cut off from its navy. Toulon came twelve years after Yorktown.

The fourth element of Napoleon's Toulon strategy was the siege of Orléans, in 1429, when Joan of Arc saved France from conquest by England. She relieved the fortress of Orléans indirectly, by taking smaller forts around the city instead of fighting over the main fortress itself.

At Toulon these four elements came together in Napoleon's mind. The contour maps showed him l'Aiguillette, a small fort around the main fortress, as at Orléans. Light cannon hauled up there could command the harbor and cut off the British army from its navy, as at Boston and Yorktown. We can see from this Toulon example that a flash of insight for strategic intuition has the same basic structure as expert intuition, except that the elements that combine in the mind come from farther afield, usually from outside the strategist's direct experience. That makes the flash of insight so much bigger when the pieces come together. Napoleon had never fought a battle like Toulon, but he was able to find on the shelves of his mind a set of elements that solved in previous battles different pieces of the Toulon problem. The combination was new, but the elements that made up the combination were not.

After Toulon, Napoleon rose quickly through the ranks of the French army. In 1796 he took up the same command as the general who laughed in his face at Toulon. He now led the army in open battle across the Italian border, against a larger force of Italians and Austrians. This time he took his strategic idea from a campaign by Frederick the Great in Poland some fifty years before. It worked. Napoleon went on to repeat his same method to conquer most of Europe. In his memoirs, Napoleon tells us how he drew from the past for his strategy:

> The principles of warfare are those that guided the great captains whose high deeds history has transmitted to us—Alexander, Hannibal, Caesar, Gustavus Adolphus, Turenne, Eugene of Savoy, Frederick the Great. . . . The history of their eighty-three campaigns would constitute a complete treatise on the art of war.[2]

We now understand what von Clausewitz tells us about coup d'oeil. He explains in four steps how coup d'oeil happens: examples from history, presence of mind, the flash of insight itself, and resolution.[3] Let's examine each of these four steps to see how it worked for the siege of Toulon.

Intelligent memory tells us that you store examples from past experience on the shelves of your brain as you go through life and learn your profession. The thick book that Napoleon carried under his arm in the film on Toulon stands in for his thorough study of military history. Expert intuition relies on your own experience, while strategic intuition draws on the experience of everyone else in the world as well. You don't just search the shelves of your own experience—you search out examples from history far and wide.

The second step in coup d'oeil is presence of mind. You clear your mind of all expectations and previous ideas of what you might do or even what your goal is. Note that the general at Toulon already had his goal: storm the main fortress by sword and bayonet. All he wanted Napoleon to do was direct the artillery to help in the storming. Instead, Napoleon freed his mind of that goal and saw a completely different end: rather than drive the English out of Toulon, they just leave.

The third step is the flash of insight itself. In a free mind selected elements from various past examples come together in a new combination. Thanks to his study of military history, Napoleon had many possible elements to draw from. But he had no idea beforehand which specific elements would come together in his mind in this particular case. There were three possible outcomes when he gazed at the map of Toulon: see that the general's plan was good, come up with a different plan, or see no way at all to get the English out of Toulon. He had no preconception about which end would prevail. Then he freed his mind, and the l'Aiguillette strategy came together in his mind.

The fourth step in coup d'oeil is resolution. This means resolve, determination, will. You not only see what to do: you also are ready to do it. The flash of insight carries with it the force of action that propels you forward. This step is very important because the first thing that happens next is the general laughs in your face. You need resolution to push on and make your coup d'oeil happen.

The four steps of coup d'oeil that von Clausewitz gives us fit our modern understanding of intelligent memory very well. These steps show how intelligent memory applies to new situations, as strategic intuition. In expert intuition you draw on what is in your mind about similar situations, while in strategic intuition you draw together selected elements from different situations in a new combination. These four elements apply to all fields of human endeavor, not just military strategy. Yet a puzzle remains: If strategic intuition is the key to strategy as von Clausewitz sees it, and von Clausewitz remains the leading authority on strategy in the modern world, then why is strategic intuition not better known in the field of strategy today?

There are two main reasons. First, we had to wait until neuroscience revealed how intelligent memory works to understand how it applies to what von Clausewitz tells us about coup d'oeil.

Second, von Clausewitz had a competitor, Baron Antoine Jomini. It was Jomini's version of strategy that first spread through military academies and later to business and other sectors. Von Clausewitz has stood the test of time, but a century ago Jomini was far better known.

Jomini's book, *Summary of the Art of War*,[4] came out in 1838, only six years after von Clausewitz's *On War*. Von Clausewitz wrote in dense German, while Jomini wrote in clear French—the language of Napoleon. Jomini was Swiss and served as a staff aide in Napoleon's army from 1804 to 1813. He used his status as an insider to claim that he told the true story of Napoleon's winning strategy.

In the fifty years after Napoleon—1820s to 1860s—a large literature arose in French to explain Napoleon's success, and Jomini's book rose quickly to the top of the heap. As the intellectual historian Edward Earle tells us, it "probably did more than any other single book to fix the great sub-divisions of modern military science for good and all and to give them common currency."[5] Those main subdivisions were strategy, tactics, and logistics. For military academies around the world Jomini provided the first common handbook for all three fields of military science.

Where von Clausewitz gives us strategic intuition, Jomini gives us strategic planning. Jomini tells you to first establish your base of operations, then determine an "objective point," and then choose lines of operations from the base to that point to move your army along.[6] That makes three basic steps: first you figure out where you are (Point A), then you decide where you want to be (Point B), and then you make a plan to get from Point A to Point B. You might recognize these steps as the same kind of strategic planning that businesses and other kinds of organizations engage in to this day.

Jomini's three steps of strategic planning are completely different from von Clausewitz's four steps of strategic intuition. Yet both authors claim to derive their steps from Napoleon. Can they both be right? We can boil the problem down to a battle between two words: *objective* and *decisive*. For Jomini, you win because you have greater force than your enemy at the objective point. For von Clausewitz, you win because you have greater force at the decisive point. In Jomini's strategic planning you choose your objective point first and then plan to reach it. In von Clausewitz's strategic intuition the decisive point arises as part of the picture that comes together in your mind. You do not start out with an objective point beforehand.

In the Toulon example the general had his objective point: the fortress of the city. He made a plan to march his army from A to B to take it. That's pure Jomini. In contrast, Napoleon's strategic intuition showed him a decisive point: the small fort of l'Aiguillette on a cliff overlooking the harbor. As von Clausewitz tells us, the decisive point arises as part of the coup d'oeil.

Out on the open battlefield Napoleon would move his army from place to place, looking for a decisive point to win a battle. If he did not see a decisive point, he just kept moving. Along the way he passed many key objective points that the enemy assumed he was trying to take. For example, in his Italian campaign after Toulon, he went right past the key cities of Turin and Milan because he did not see how to win there. Confused, the enemy came out to chase him. In a series of six battles in odd and unimportant locations, Napoleon beat them.

In his memoirs, Napoleon's own words support von Clausewitz's decisive point over Jomini's objective point:

> The art of war consists, with a numerically inferior army, in always having larger forces than the enemy at the point which must be attacked or defended ... it is an intuitive way of acting which properly constitutes the genius of war.[7]

Napoleon wanted superior strength wherever he fought the battle. That was his decisive point. He did not set out an objective point and march his army to it.

Yet Jomini's three steps were much easier than von Clausewitz's four steps for generals of the day to understand. The American army especially embraced Jomini's three steps, first in the original French and then in Henry Halleck's English translation. When the American army split to fight the Civil War, both sides followed Jomini. This explains the massive bloody battles where both sides picked the same *objective point* and marched head-on to take it. The same kind of battle dominated World War I as well. Only in World War II did an American general, George Patton, master von Clausewitz's decisive point instead.

Patton was the most successful American battlefield general in World War II. He used his tanks like Napoleon's cavalry. In a comment on his method, Patton tells us that an officer must study history to become

> so thoroughly conversant with all sorts of military possibilities that whenever an occasion arises he has at hand without effort on his part a parallel. To attain this end I think it is necessary for a man to begin to read military history in its earliest and hence crudest form and to follow it down in natural sequence permitting his mind to grow with his subject until he can grasp without effort the most abstruse question of the science of war.[8]

Here we see that Patton put so many examples from history on the shelves of his brain that he could draw on them quickly. Expert intuition shades into strategic intuition: examples beyond his own experience become as familiar to him as his own experience. For instance, while the British army fought the Germans straight on to take Messina, the capital of Sicily, Patton saw a way around instead, via the town of Agrigento, because Carthage invaded that way in 406 B.C. Patton's coup d'oeil shifted him from the *objective point* of Messina to the *decisive point* of Agrigento.

In modern times Jomini's three steps from A to B still reign supreme over von Clausewitz's four steps of coup d'oeil. Strategic planning in the Jomini tradition is commonplace in business and other kinds of organizations around the world. There are countless textbooks of strategic planning today, all in the Jomini tradition. Military academies and universities assign von Clausewitz's *On War* for its philosophy and theory, but for the practice of strategy they follow Jomini's handbook without even knowing it.

There is one new field that honors von Clausewitz as one of its founders: nonlinear studies. Scholars of nonlinearity study phenomena of irregular patterns that defy prediction with ordinary tools of analysis. Mathematics and physics dominate the field, but social science and even philosophy join in too. The Santa Fe Institute is perhaps the leading center of nonlinear studies, but there are many others: for example, at Cambridge, Duke, Free University of Brussels, Australian National University, Los Alamos National Laboratory, and Hong Kong Baptist University. In social science we get books like *Nonlinear Dynamics in Human Behavior* by W. Sulis and Allan Combs, *Nonlinear Models for Archaeology and Anthropology: Continuing the Revolution* by Christopher Beekman and William Baden, and *A Thousand Years of Nonlinear History* by Manuel De Landa.[9]

On von Clausewitz we can look to a 1992 article by Alan Beyerchen, "Clausewitz, Nonlinearity, and the Unpredictability of War."[10] According to von Clausewitz the outcome of a war depends on what happens during the war, which in turn depends on the general's coup d'oeil. You cannot predict the outcome beforehand. Strategic intuition is very much a nonlinear discipline. Von Clausewitz overturned the idea of linear strategy in war, as Kuhn overturned the idea of linear development in science, and they both put flashes of insight as the key mechanism that creates the twists and turns. Many aspects of human life are predictable, but what comes together in somebody's mind will likely never be one of them.

We will return to the question of nonlinear dynamics in a later chapter on business strategy. Many linear analytical methods try to predict the outcome of various business situations, for very high stakes indeed. But the real prize comes from nonlinear outcomes: disruptive changes that transform industries or create new ones. We will see this in action in the computer revolution from Microsoft to Google, where strategic intuition played the same role that Kuhn discovered in the scientific revolution from Copernicus to Newton. And rather than abandon linear methods—you cannot avoid them in modern business—we will see how to adapt them to take account of strategic intuition.

On the military side the coup d'oeil of von Clausewitz came full circle in 2005, when the U.S. Army commissioned a study on how strategic intuition applies to their current procedures.[11] Sure enough, the study found that Jomini's, not von Clausewitz's, steps still dominate the army's formal methods of strategy to this day. Yet in practice, officers in the field tend to apply von Clausewitz's steps. Klein for one would find this hardly surprising at all. It's the manuals that need to change, to encourage rather than contradict strategic intuition.

[6]

Warrior Buddha

The Path to Beginner's Mind

We now turn to Asia, where we find a tradition of military strategy very different from the formal scholarship of Carl von Clausewitz. Strategy in Asia comes in the form of ancient philosophy: Hindu, Buddhist, and Tao. In content, though, East and West have much in common. We find strategic intuition in both. The form is different, but the idea is the same. For example, Buddhists aim to be one with the universe, and it's a flash of insight that makes it happen.

Military strategy and Asian philosophy might seem to be an odd match. In the West, Asian philosophy has a reputation for meditation and peace, not for armed conflict. Mahatma Gandhi was a Hindu holy man who preached nonviolence during India's struggle for independence. The Dalai Lama of Tibet is a Buddhist holy man who preaches nonviolence today. Yoga and Zen are popular methods of relaxation. What do they have to do with war?

There is a well-known modern tradition with a direct link between military strategy and Asian philosophy: Asian martial arts. Their names give it away: judo, kendo, aikido, and even karate (its correct name is *karatedo*). The word *do* means Tao. In China Tao went from a folk religion to a more formal spiritual philosophy around 400 B.C. In India Buddhism arose as an offshoot of Hinduism at about the same time and spread from India to China after A.D. 100. In China Buddhism mixed with Tao to form Zen Buddhism. Asian martial arts adopted the philosophy of Zen, with Tao as its central idea.

Asian military strategy shows us strategic intuition in a highly philosophical form. Strategic intuition is very much a philosophy of action for any domain, military or otherwise. Strategic intuition requires a mental discipline that Asian philosophy teaches. The Hindu, Tao, and Buddhist traditions are very old and very diverse: at one extreme they are religions, and at the other extreme they are practical methods of war. Here we study the practical end of the spectrum, where a flash of insight leads to a useful course of action. But even this "unholy" practical side has a spiritual angle, not as religion but as inner peace.

We start with the key writings of these Asian philosophies, to see where strategic intuition appears in them. We look especially for intelligent memory and the four steps of von Clausewitz: examples from history, presence of mind, the flash of insight, and resolution. We pay special attention to the great contribution these philosophies make about *presence of mind* in particular. In Zen, which combines elements of the other Asian philosophies, we encounter presence of mind as *beginner's mind*. We conclude with a practical method for adapting the strategic elements of these ancient philosophies to modern problems and situations.

Four key classics shed light on strategic intuition in Asian philosophy: Sun Tzu's *The Art of War* (450 B.C.) and Lao Tze's *Tao te Ching* (400 B.C.) from China; *Bhagavad Gita* (400 B.C.)—of no known author—from India; and Miyamoto Musashi's *Book of Five Rings* (A.D. 1645) from Japan. *The Art of War* applies a practical version of Tao to military strategy. *Tao te Ching* presents an even purer philosophy of Tao for political strategy and life in general. *Bhagavad Gita* both presents a concise statement of Hindu philosophy and serves as a guide to strategy in life and war through the mental discipline of Yoga. *Book of Five Rings* is a guide to Zen as a mental discipline for samurai warriors in medieval Japan.

These four classics present a philosophy of action that applies most directly to war but also to life in general. Despite their practical purpose they read more like von Clausewitz's strategic philosophy than Jomini's handbook. As von Clausewitz wrote in the tradition of German Idealists, the various authors of these Asian classics wrote in their local traditions of spiritual teaching. Their great antiquity makes them even more remote than von Clausewitz from the modern science of the brain. You cannot just read them once and get the idea. You must also understand the traditions they come from—Hindu, Tao, and Buddhist—to gauge what these classics are trying to convey.[1]

The summary that follows derives from all four classics and all four traditions, pieced together as a single whole. Each tradition features a whole world of ideas, and each of these classics amounts to but one part of its world, and within each part we narrow our search to their implications for strategy. As a result this summary covers only a small corner of the vast tapestry that these Asian philosophies have woven through the ages. We will only take a narrow view and look for the basic elements of strategic intuition, especially presence of mind, in the spirit of von Clausewitz.

Within our four traditions—Hindu, Tao, Buddhist, and Zen— one historic flash of insight stands out above all others: how Buddha achieved enlightenment. Although Buddha never wrote anything down, the historical record convinces scholars that the basic story of Buddha's life is true. His flash of insight will be our entry into strategic intuition as Asian philosophy presents it.

Buddha means "enlightened one." He gained that name after his flash of insight around 500 B.C. He was born with the name Siddhartha Gautama, in what was then northern India and today is Nepal. His father was head of a small tribal kingdom and his mother a princess from a neighboring kingdom. As a prince of the realm Siddhartha grew up in luxury. At sixteen he married a cousin. At twenty-nine he left his family to wander the countryside in search of enlightenment.

Such wandering seekers were common in Hindu tradition. After six years Siddhartha achieved his breakthrough. From then on he devoted his life to teaching others what he discovered, still as a wanderer. He traveled far and wide across northern India. After forty-five years of teaching, at the age of eighty, Siddhartha died. His many followers carried on his teachings. He was the original Buddha that they all tried to emulate, to reach enlightenment in the same way as Buddha himself achieved it.

Scholars agree on this basic outline of Buddha's life. Beyond that, over the centuries, many legends arose to fill in the details. The most important part of Buddha's tale is his breakthrough, and here we must rely on the legends. These legends disagree on many details, but within the many versions we find a common thread that gives us the essence of Buddhist philosophy and leads us to strategic intuition.

The story of Siddhartha's breakthrough begins with his state of mind before he set off in search of enlightenment. As a boy he never left the palace. His father kept all things unpleasant well out of sight. Then one day, when Siddhartha was twenty-nine, curiosity took him beyond the palace walls. He saw a crippled old man. For the first time Siddhartha realized that suffering, not princely pleasure, was the normal state of the world. Everyone, himself included, was one day bound to die. This struck the young prince as a terrible blow. He went outside the palace again and again and found more suffering wherever he looked. Siddhartha fell into an abyss of despair. Finally he left the palace and set out into the wider world, with nothing but the clothes on his back and the solemn intention to seek relief from his pain.

In those days Hindu gurus wandered the countryside teaching different methods to achieve enlightenment. Siddhartha went from guru to guru. He learned each set of techniques and practiced them. Some gurus made him meditate and chant magic words. Others taught him special Yoga poses. Still others had him eat only certain foods, or nothing at all. In each case Siddhartha learned the techniques, practiced them, and found they did not work. Each guru was very popular, with plenty of followers who did exactly what the guru said. The most popular gurus were charismatic, and their followers formed a community around them.

But that was not what Siddhartha was after. So he moved on to the next guru and the next and the next.

After six years he gave up on gurus and resolved to find enlightenment on his own. Outside the town of Gaya he sat down at the foot of a fig tree and meditated for a long time. The Hindu god of evil, Mara, tried to tempt him away with earthly pleasures and scare him away with earthly terrors. But in the end Gautama reached enlightenment. It came in a flash of insight. He saw all at once in his mind the answer to human suffering: the Four Noble Truths of Buddhism. For a long time he just sat there, contemplating what he had seen and what he should do about it. Then he rose and went out to teach it to others.[2]

Here are Buddha's Four Noble Truths: (1) life is suffering, (2) desire causes suffering, (3) it is possible to end desire, and (4) the way to end desire is the Eightfold Path—Right View, Right Intention, Right Speech, Right Action, Right Livelihood, Right Effort, Right Mindfulness, and Right Concentration. These Four Noble Truths amount to a personal discipline of thought and action that follows not your own desires but the forces at play in the world around you. You *go with the flow* instead of *get what you want*. Enlightenment has nothing to do with the magic words or the poses or the diets that the gurus taught him. The answer was there all along inside Siddhartha's mind.

Every Buddhist aims to achieve the same stroke of enlightenment as Siddhartha, the original Buddha, under the fig tree of Gaya. Scholars find the Four Noble Truths in Hindu texts that existed long before Buddha was born. But they appear there mixed up with many other Hindu ideas. Buddha was the first to select and combine these four ideas in just that way. The Four Noble Truths are simpler than any other summary of Hindu thought, and they are completely within the power of any individual. You do not need a scholar to interpret sacred texts for you or a guru to give you chants or poses or diets. Through mental discipline you can learn them on your own, just like Buddha did. And it is no accident that a Hindu god, Mara, tried to keep Buddha from enlightenment. Buddhism is not against gods—some Buddhist sects pray to them as to saints—but they are not your means to enlightenment. You achieve enlightenment on your own.

Buddha's epiphany about the Four Noble Truths stands out as one of history's great flashes of insight. It fits how von Clausewitz describes a coup d'oeil: "the rapid discovery of a truth which to the ordinary mind is either not visible at all or only becomes so after long examination and reflection."[3] Buddha's examples from history were elements of Hindu philosophy plus the Hindu tradition of wandering gurus. His presence of mind came from years of mental discipline. And the flash of insight gave him great resolution to devote the rest of his life to teaching the same thing to others.

Note that von Clausewitz calls what you see in a coup d'oeil a "truth." He does not believe you can prove that truth to anyone but yourself. That's why you need resolution. Buddha's flash of insight showed him the Four Noble Truths at once. Note too that von Clausewitz tells us that an *ordinary mind* can't see what the coup d'oeil reveals, at least not nearly as fast. Buddha gives us instruction in the mental discipline to turn an ordinary mind into one that sees a coup d'oeil. In a spiritual sense the Four Noble Truths lead to enlightenment, while in a secular sense they prepare your mind for coup d'oeil.

We now recall Thomas Kuhn's flash of insight, where the pieces of Aristotle's laws of physics came together in his mind as *truth*, when he in fact had been working on the problem of how Aristotle could be so wrong. Such a huge flash of insight usually means you change direction: from disproving Aristotle to accepting him, from following gurus to do-it-yourself. Yet Buddha's enlightenment is more than a classic example of strategic intuition in action. His insight itself gives us further guidance on how strategic intuition works. The Four Noble Truths amount to a mental discipline of the third element of von Clausewitz's coup d'oeil: presence of mind.

Buddha called his teaching *Dharma*. It is the path you tread when you understand the Four Noble Truths. Dharma is an old Hindu term that the *Bhagavad Gita* uses in contrast to Karma.

When Buddhism spread to China and mixed with Tao to form Zen, Dharma gave way to its Chinese equivalent: Tao. Tao is the path of Dharma. It means both the particular right path—your strategy—that you follow in any circumstance and the general discipline of always following the right path. You follow Dharma–Tao in a particular moment but also throughout your life. Rather than pick either of these names, let's call it by the usual translation of "Tao" into English: the Way.

Above all, the Way avoids conflict. For the spiritual side of Buddhism this is easy to understand. The Four Noble Truths conquer desire, and without desire you have nothing to fight about. Yet Sun Tzu's version of Tao is called *The Art of War*, and the Asian *do*s are martial arts, and *Book of Five Rings* is a manual for samurai warriors. How can the Way both avoid conflict and help you fight better? The answer is: presence of mind.

The Way avoids a certain kind of conflict: Karma versus Dharma. You must find a Dharma that fits your Karma. Your Karma is the full set of circumstances the universe presents to you that are beyond your control. Your Dharma is your own set of thoughts and actions. These are within your control. You find your Way by sorting out what exactly is within your control and what is not, and then finding the particular thoughts and actions within your control that best fit what is beyond your control rather than what you most desire. You do what you can, not what you want. Your Dharma follows your Karma, not your desires.

Let's go back to the example of Napoleon. He was the general in command at sixty battles. How can we possibly say he avoided conflict? And his ambition led him to conquer Europe. Did he really not desire that? In his memoirs Napoleon gives us these glimpses into his state of mind:

I never truly was my own master but was always ruled by circumstances.

The greater one is, the less will he must have. He depends on events and circumstances.

I had few really definite ideas, and the reason for this was that, instead of obstinately seeking to control circumstances, I obeyed them.

The fact was that I was not a master of my actions, because I was not so insane as to attempt to bend events to conform to my policies. On the contrary, I bent my policies to accord with the unforeseen shape of events.[4]

Napoleon was a master of finding his Way amid the forces arrayed against him. He passed up more battles than he fought, looking for only those he could win. He assessed his Karma and found a Dharma to fit. Only once did he lose his Way: in 1812 he thought he was so powerful that he could not lose. Instead of his usual unpredictable strategy he took the Jomini approach and marched straight to Moscow. It was his greatest mistake and led to his eventual downfall.

We find a similar view of the Way in *The Art of War*. Here are excerpts where Sun Tzu's philosophical guidance echoes Napoleon's mental state:

Do not engage an enemy advancing with well-ordered banners, nor one whose formations are in impressive array. This is control of the factor of changing circumstances.

Experts in war depend especially on opportunity and expediency.

Now an army must be likened to water, for just as flowing water avoids the heights and hastens to the lowlands, so an army avoids strength and strikes weakness.[5]

Dharma flows like water around the rocks of Karma. This is the essence of Asian martial arts. You practice your moves so they become second nature to you, and then you free your mind and let the circumstances of the battle guide your actions in a series of flashes of insight that show you the Way. Such flashes have the same character as Buddha's enlightenment—or your own—except on a smaller scale. You must free your mind of all desire as to what kind of battle you want it to be and of all expectation of what kind of battle you think it will be. You must conform to Karma, not fight it. You cannot even desire to win the battle because halfway through the Way might lead to retreat instead.

Buddha's Four Noble Truths provide the mental training to find your Dharma in all situations. The result is presence of mind. Von Clausewitz tells us that a strategist must master presence of mind, but he gives us no guidance on how to achieve that. Presence of mind is not like examples from history where simple study does the trick. Presence of mind requires constant practice, so you expect the unexpected every waking moment. Your mind is always ready. Asian philosophy of action, from Buddha through *Book of Five Rings*, provides the Way to make presence of mind a permanent feature of how you think.

In all walks of life one of the greatest obstacles to achieving presence of mind is mastery of your particular craft. It is easy to fall prey to overconfidence. On a larger scale this overconfidence can lead to something similar to Napoleon's march to Moscow. On a smaller scale you jump to conclusions too fast. This is because you use expert intuition in situations that call for strategic intuition. You think a situation looks familiar, but you miss the elements that make it different. Expertise can give you a false sense of mastery. What you need instead is the Zen discipline of *beginner's mind* in every situation.

Beginner's mind is exactly von Clausewitz's presence of mind. It does not mean that you fail to master your craft. It is a step beyond mastery, when you clear your mind of all you know the moment you step onto the field of battle.[6] Otherwise, you carry thoughts into the battle based on the wrong Karma. You cannot fully know what forces are in play in the battle—what moves you will need, what goal you must set—until you reach the moment of the battle itself. And as all life is a battle—that is, a field for action of some kind—you aim to achieve beginner's mind as a permanent mental state.

Buddha himself achieved beginner's mind under the fig tree of Gaya. After Mara tried to lure him away with earthly pleasures and scare him away with earthly terrors, the evil god asked, "And who will witness that you are worthy to reach enlightenment?" Buddha reached one hand down to the ground and said, "The earth is my witness." That was it. In a flash he merged with the universe, through the touch of the earth on his finger. Many statues of Buddha show the moment enlightenment came to him. He sits with legs crossed and one hand in his lap. The other hand rests over one knee, with one finger touching the earth.

This is a wonderful image of beginner's mind, where you open yourself to the universe around you. Strategic intuition is an internal discipline of external inspiration. Your brain combines elements it takes in from outside you. The examples from history that a coup d'oeil combines come from that outside world. You connect to that world, as Buddha touched the earth. That grounds your coup d'oeil in reality. You let the examples from history flow into you, combine, and flow out as action that moves the world forward, and this action immediately becomes part of Karma, which you and everyone else take into account for the next moment of Dharma. When you follow the Way, Karma and Dharma are not in conflict. One flows into the other, on and on through time.

In the same manner Copernicus connected with Aristarchus, the inventors of trigonometry, and the hundreds of astronomers through the ages who made the observations of heavenly bodies he used in his calculations. Napoleon connected with the inventors of contour maps, the metal workers who made the light cannon, George Washington at Yorktown, and Joan of Arc at Orléans. And each of these sources connected to their own sources, who in turn connected to their own sources, and so on back through the ages. Each new flash of insight draws elements from Karma to become a new Dharma, which becomes part of the Karma for future Dharma to draw on.

In the discipline of beginner's mind the hardest part is taking your mind off what you want. Buddha put this problem right up front in his Noble Truths: all unhappiness comes from frustrated desire. Anger, jealousy, regret, fear, contempt, grief, disappointment, and anxiety—all negative emotions—arise from wanting something you could not have in the past or cannot have in the present or future. In the field of strategy we translate unhappiness as failure, when a course of action fails to achieve the intended goal. All failed strategies come from picking the wrong combination of actions for the wrong goal. Success comes from picking the right combination for the right goal.

Now, let's return to Jomini versus von Clausewitz. Jomini tells you to pick your desired objective and march toward it. Von Clausewitz tells you to wait for the decisive point when a combination of past examples can achieve a worthy goal. Jomini tells you to control the flow. Von Clausewitz tells you to go with the flow. Asian philosophy gives us more detail on what that flow is and how you can train your mind to follow it.

To reach your goal you give up your goal. To achieve your desire you suspend desire. You open your mind in order to let the best possible actions from the past combine to reach the best possible goal in the future. You touch the earth, and the answer comes.

But how can you go through life without any goal to start with? Surely Napoleon's starting goal was to defeat the enemy. Buddha's starting goal was to find enlightenment. The strategy you decide on just gives you a specific goal to attain your general goal. Doesn't the general goal come first?

Not quite. What made Napoleon think in the first place that he could possibly reach his goal of defeating the enemy? What made Buddha think that he could find enlightenment? In each case the goal arose because the strategist thought it was possible for him to attain that goal in the time and place he found himself. The Karma offered elements of that particular Dharma to carry forward. Astronomy was a common pursuit among church scholars in Copernicus's time. Napoleon's family sent him to military school at a young age, and the French Revolution happened just as he graduated from the military school. Buddha saw wandering Hindu gurus who claimed to have achieved enlightenment, so he set off to imitate them.

In all these cases the general goal arose from Karma—the world outside the strategist's control. Copernicus, Napoleon, and Buddha chose general goals that Karma made possible: a career in science, a career in the military, and a career in spirituality. But might they have chosen some other general goal that Karma also made possible? In keeping with their time and place might Copernicus have studied medicine instead of philosophy, might Napoleon have been a royalist, or might Buddha have stayed an Indian prince and succeeded his father as king? The answer is: yes. If they had done that, they and history would have turned out different.

The lesson here is that your general goal can arise from a general understanding of the Karma you face. But you must have some general notion of your course of action too, or else you are seeking the impossible. Copernicus, Napoleon, and Buddha saw a general path for success as part of setting general goals in the first place. That's why a strategy includes both a goal and a course of action to get there. A strategy is Dharma—a Way of action toward a goal.

In the end it's a matter of free will: many Dharmas are possible, and you pick one. That's true both for a general goal and for the flash of insight that shows you a more specific goal, which you remain free to ignore. For example, your company can pick an overall mission, or a person can choose a career, that fits better or worse the circumstances you face. The same is true for any other organization and any other decision in life—a nonprofit agency, love, marriage, government, children, you name it. You want to find the general Ways that can lead you to specific Ways for the greatest happiness and success.

In the chapters that follow we study these modern fields of action and how we find our Way in each one. In every case we seek variations on Buddha's finger touching the earth: how to ground our strategy in what is possible, through connection to those examples from history we might combine to reach some worthy goal.

7

Gates and the Google Guys Go for It

Strategic Innovation in Business

Our next field of action is business strategy. Here we find a recent example of major change that matches Kuhn's scientific revolution from Copernicus to Newton: the revolution in personal computers—PCs—from Microsoft to Google. The scientific revolution from Copernicus to Newton took 170 years, yet the PC revolution from Microsoft to Google took only 23 years. That speaks volumes about developments in modern business. Both revolutions changed the world, but the second one much faster than the first.

The great success of the PC revolution serves as an outstanding case of what all businesses seek to some degree: strategic innovation. Not all innovation leads to victory. An innovation is strategic when it takes your strategy in a new direction that pays off in the end. The PC revolution featured strategic innovation on the part of big-time winners like Microsoft and Google but also of second-tier firms like Apple and IBM. This chapter asks how the leaders of these firms came up with the winning ideas at the heart of their strategic innovations. Sure enough, we find that the answer is strategic intuition.

We then compare what strategic intuition tells us about strategic innovation with the leading conventional model of business strategy. That model comes from Michael Porter of Harvard Business School. His two books from the 1980s, *Competitive Strategy* and *Competitive Advantage*, still dominate the field today.[1] Porter was the first to apply economic analysis to business strategy as practical tools for managers. You find his ideas and methods in strategy courses at business schools, in techniques that consultants and company staff use for strategy, and even in the language people use as they talk about business strategy. At last count Porter is the world's most cited business authority, on the Internet and in the academic and popular press.[2] Sure enough, strategic intuition offers a very different view of strategic innovation from Porter's. Yet we conclude with a way to reconcile the two, thanks to the work of two other leading economists, Daniel Kahneman and Joseph Schumpeter, whose work helps sort out the proper role of analysis and intuition in strategic thinking. In the end, business can benefit from both analytical methods like Porter's and strategic intuition, as long as we keep straight what each is able to do.

Let's turn to our first example, Microsoft, to see how Bill Gates arrived at his big idea. It was Gates who foresaw that PCs would be a huge business and that all those machines would need software. He led Microsoft to dominate the PC business, from 1975 to this day. In a 1995 book, *The Road Ahead*,[3] he explains how he did it. All in all Gates makes an excellent subject for a case study of strategic innovation in action.

Gates began his career not in PCs but with something bigger: the minicomputer. In the early 1970s he and his friend Paul Allen learned how to program their high school's PDP-8 minicomputer from DEC—the Digital Equipment Corporation. The PDP-8 first came out in 1965 and cost $18,000. It was the cheapest and smallest computer on the market and the first commercially successful stand-alone computer to spread beyond big companies. Gates and Allen used BASIC to program their school's PDP-8: BASIC was a simple computer language that two Dartmouth professors wrote in 1964 to make it easier to teach students how to program computers. Big computers used the more complicated computer languages like COBOL and FORTRAN.

Allen graduated in 1971 and went to Washington State University in Pullman, a long bus ride away, across the state. In 1972 Intel's new 8008 microprocessor came out. It was as if the entire PDP-8 shrank down to just that one chip—almost. Gates and Allen tried to fit BASIC on the chip, but the 8008 was too small. Instead they wrote an even simpler program for the 8008, combined it with a PDP-8 machine, and formed a company to sell it. The machine counted traffic, so they called the company Traf-O-Data.

They sold exactly zero machines.

Gates graduated and went off to college at Harvard. To stay in touch Allen dropped out of college and drove across the country to take a job at Honeywell in Boston. He worked on programming a new line of minicomputers to compete with the PDP-8. The next spring Intel put out a new chip: the 8080. Gates and Allen studied the manual to see if BASIC would fit. The answer was yes. So they wrote to all the big computer companies with an offer to write a BASIC program for them to fit on the new Intel chip. Not a single one said yes.

Gates recalls:

By December of 1974 we were pretty discouraged. I was planning to go fly home to Seattle for the holidays, and Paul was going to stay on in Boston. On an achingly cold Massachusetts morning a few days before I left, Paul rushed me to the Harvard Square newsstand to show me the January issue of *Popular Electronics*.[4]

As Robert Cringely explains in his detailed history of the PC era, *Accidental Empires*: "Like the Buddha, Gates's enlightenment came in a flash."[5] Allen was just walking by the newsstand on his way to Gates's dorm room. A magazine cover caught his eye. He brought Gates back to the same spot to have the same insight.

The magazine had on its cover a new computer, the Altair, from a tiny company in New Mexico called MITS. The Altair was small enough to fit on a desk. It cost $397. Inside was an 8080 chip.

Gates recalls:

When we saw that, panic set in. "Oh no! It's happening without us. People are going to write real software for this chip!" The future was staring us in the face from the cover of a magazine. It wasn't going to wait for us. Getting in on the first stages of the PC revolution looked like the opportunity of a lifetime, and we seized it.[6]

They called up MITS and said they were working on a BASIC program that would fit the Altair. MITS said they were interested, so Gates and Allen worked feverishly over the next six weeks. They did not have an Altair to work on. Neither did MITS have any to sell them: the picture on the magazine cover was an empty box. MITS has completed the Altair prototype but had none to sell yet. Instead, MITS sent Gates and Allen an Altair manual to work from. To simulate an Altair, Allen used the manual to program a PDP-8 in the Harvard computer laboratory. Meanwhile, Gates worked on adapting BASIC.

At the end of six weeks Allen took the software to MITS in Albuquerque. For the first time he used it to program a real Altair. It worked. They won the contract.

MITS went on to ship the Altair to customers with the software that Gates and Allen wrote. Allen quit his job at Honeywell and Gates took a leave of absence from Harvard. They moved to Albuquerque and started a new company, Micro-Soft, on April 4, 1975.

So ends the first chapter of the Microsoft story. As of its founding the company had a monopoly on operating software for mass-market PCs. Over the next thirty years they preserved that monopoly, as the PC industry took off and then spread to take over the world. This first achievement—the Altair contract—was Microsoft's most important. It made them different from everyone else in the business. They essentially replicated the same contract with more and more computer makers across the globe.

The Altair contract was a clear case of strategic intuition in action. Gates and Allen put together four existing elements they did not invent: the Altair, its 8080 chip, BASIC, and the PDP-8. Their presence of mind let the new combination come together as a flash of insight that changed their goals, to establish a software company for microcomputers, which they had never thought of before. One minute Gates was preparing to fly home to Seattle for the holidays, with Allen staying in Boston at his Honeywell job, and the next minute they were off in a new direction. Their resolution carried them through those torrid six weeks to win the contract and on through the following decades.

After the Altair, Gates became a visionary. He explains:

We believed that there would be computers everywhere because computing power would be cheap and great new software would take advantage of it. We set up shop betting on cheap computing power and producing software when nobody else was.[7]

Strategic intuition gave Gates this vision. He did not have the vision before the Altair. In the Jomini view your vision comes first and then comes your course of action to reach it. In the von Clausewitz view, the flash of insight comes first and then comes the vision for where it can take you. This is a key feature of strategic innovation in business: it gives you a new vision.

Gates did not have a software vision before the Altair, but he did foresee computers getting better, smaller, and cheaper. Yet plenty of people thought the same thing. Gordon Moore, a founder of Intel, noted in 1965 that processing power was doubling every two years, and he predicted it would continue to do so. That prediction became widely known as Moore's law, and it turned out to be right. The PDP-8 minicomputer—also from 1965—was the first big step in that direction. Gates caught the bug in high school:

Despite its limitations, the PDP-8 inspired us to indulge in the dream that one day millions of individuals could possess their own computers.[8]

The founder of MITS, Ed Roberts, had the same dream. So did Honeywell, who hired Allen for precisely that reason. But if Gates was no more visionary about smaller computers than many others in the field, was he ahead of the pack for a vision of new PC functions—user-friendly applications with words, pictures, spreadsheets, and so on? Let's ask him:

> When Paul Allen and I saw that picture of the first Altair computer, we could only guess at the wealth of applications it would inspire. We knew applications would be developed but we didn't know what they would be. Some were predictable—for example, programs that would let a PC function as the terminal for a mainframe computer—but the most important applications, such as VisiCalc spreadsheets, were unexpected.[9]

At the time of the Altair, Gates thought that computers were meant for data processing. And he assumed that the mainframe itself would always do most of the work. Note the "predictable" applications: the PC as a mainframe terminal. That's what Gates thought the Altair and its descendants were meant for. Now note the "unexpected" applications: VisiCalc spreadsheets and other "most important" ones, which later became the programs that made the PC so popular. Others—not Gates and Allen—later developed these programs. Microsoft then scooped these programs up and integrated them into its software. Before the Altair, Gates's view of what computers would do in the future was no more advanced than that of Allen's bosses at Honeywell or Roberts at MITS.

If Gates's pre-Altair vision of the PC was not innovative, surely he was the first to think of monopolizing software for PCs. But again we ask where this idea came from: his vision of the future or his flash of insight when he saw the Altair? Before the Altair, Gates and Allen had formed Traf-O-Data to sell hardware, not software. In that respect they were like everyone else. When Traf-O-Data failed, Gates recalls:

> We were disappointed, but we still believed that our future, even if it was not to be in hardware, might have something to do with microprocessors.[10]

This is hardly a manifesto for software. After Traf-O-Data Gates and Allen gave up on a hardware machine but kept their eye on Intel's 8080 chip—hardware again. They thought that minicomputer makers would snap it up—and they did—so they offered to write BASIC software for it. This was a very good idea, but Gates and Allen did not set up a software company to do it. Certainly they had no dreams of a software monopoly. Computer companies hired plenty of staff and consultants to write software for their machines, and that's all Gates and Allen offered to do. It was completely in keeping with normal practice at the time. When no one hired them, they gave up and went back to what they were doing: Harvard for Gates and programming Honeywell minicomputers for Allen. They had the idea for a software company for microcomputers only on seeing the Altair and the chance to combine existing elements to make such a company happen.

Nor did Gates and Allen have unusual skill in writing software. They were both good programmers but not great ones: neither of them ever wrote a software program that countless others at the time were not also perfectly qualified to do. BASIC itself was a widespread program that thousands of programmers already knew. The vision of Gates and Allen certainly did not come from greater ability in their field.

Meanwhile, it was Ed Roberts of MITS—not Gates and Allen—who had the idea to put the 8080 chip into something smaller than a minicomputer: the Altair microcomputer. The term *microcomputer* did not even exist yet. The magazine cover announced the Altair as the "World's First Mini-computer Kit to Rival Commercial Models." It was smaller and cheaper than other minicomputers but not more powerful. When the Altair came out Gates and Allen were right in the mainstream of the minicomputer world. Right up to the moment they saw the Altair on the magazine cover there was nothing to indicate that Gates and Allen had any different vision or goal or course of action than the thousands of others who understood that computers were getting smaller and cheaper and better, as Moore's law predicted in 1965.

What was very different—and what changed the world and their personal lives—is what happened next. When Gates and Allen saw the Altair, the same thought flashed in their minds: write a BASIC program for the Altair's 8080 chip, using Harvard's PDP-8 computer. In Jomini terms their new vision was the Altair as the first popular microcomputer, the way the PDP-8 was the world's first popular minicomputer. Their goal was to win a contract for the Altair software, and their course of action was to adapt a PDP-8 and BASIC, which is something they had already done. Jomini planning is perfectly fine, after strategic intuition. You plan only after you have an idea. Of course you march from A to B once your flash of insight shows you A and shows you B and shows you a way to get from one to the other.

Before the Altair, Gates and Allen had a vision of the computer industry that was not at all unusual. Their flash of insight combined elements available to everyone else in the field. So why did they, and nobody else, make the right combination? Here we come back to Karma, Dharma, and free will. We can certainly see that Karma was in their favor. Their high school could afford a PDP-8 because their school was private and wealthy and the parents of both Gates and Allen had the means to send them there. It was luck that they knew each other and got along so well. Then Harvard, not Gates or Allen, bought a PDP-8 for its computer laboratory. Intel built the 8080 chip. MITS built the Altair computer and rushed the Altair to market without any software. All these circumstances beyond their control gave Gates and Allen an advantage.

But the circumstances were favorable for many other people too. It was Gates's and Allens's Dharma that set them apart. When the Altair came out they alone saw the combination that led to Microsoft, and they followed through with tremendous intelligence and resolve. Their Karma gave them equal possibilities to many others in the field, but their Dharma gave them their strategy. A flash of strategic intuition showed them the way to go. That was how they stood out from the crowd. Gates ended up standing even higher than Allen. Gates wrote more of the actual Altair BASIC code, because Allen still had a full-time job at Honeywell. As a result Gates took 64 percent of the company and Allen 36 percent. That split made Gates, not Allen, the head of Microsoft and eventually the famous figure we know today.

Of course, Gates and Allen were also free to ignore their strategic intuition. Yet they felt the force of Karma around them: "Oh no!" they cried. "It's happening without us." A flash of insight comes with its own timing: you feel you must do it now. Later is too late. A particular Dharma fits a particular Karma at a particular moment in time. In the same way, Napoleon could not return to the same battlefield and fight the same battle again. The universe moves on, and you must conform to it. With your free will, you can choose to make your Dharma follow the Karma that you face.

By setting up Microsoft as a business separate from MITS, Gates and Allen freed themselves to sell software to other companies too. Initially there was plenty of work at MITS, which sold ten thousand Altairs in the first year. Right away other companies came out with clones. Commodore was one of the first cloners, and Microsoft sold them a version of Altair BASIC. Another was Apple, who added a keyboard and screen. *Byte* magazine called the Apple I the first "personal computer." MITS sued Microsoft to claim partial ownership of Altair BASIC, but Microsoft won. Through the late 1970s the market flooded with many different PCs, most of which used Microsoft BASIC. By the time IBM joined in, with its 1981 PC 5150, Microsoft BASIC was the standard software for PCs.

Like MITS, IBM rushed to market without any software. Microsoft was the industry leader in software, so it was no surprise they won the IBM contract. After IBM came IBM clones—especially Compaq in 1984 and Dell in 1986. They all used the same basic components as the IBM, especially the Intel chip and Microsoft software. The Intel–Microsoft standard took over the industry, so that machines all over the world could exchange programs easily. Eventually the worldwide demands of compatibility turned Microsoft into the greatest monopoly in the history of the world.

We can now see that Microsoft's leading role in the great leap from mainframe computers to PCs came from strategic intuition: Gates and Allen combined existing elements in a flash of insight to win the Altair contract and then carried that same insight forward through the following thirty years. Strategic innovation featured strategic intuition at its turning point: when the winning idea arose in the strategist's mind. Gates and Allen had the same analysis as many others before the Altair. After the Altair they were the first to make a new analysis that featured common software across machines. But that new analysis did not come about through the old analysis: it happened as a flash of insight, just like Kuhn describes for science.

Strategic intuition played a key role throughout the PC revolution. VisiCalc came from three previous elements: the mouse, a fighter plane dashboard, and the calculator. E-mail combined an existing internal message routine with the existing Internet protocol.[11] And so on through the strategic innovations that led to PCs supplanting mainframes as the basic machine for office work. Now you had a computer not in a big central room in the basement but on everyone's desk, and then in homes, in stores, and just about everywhere else you can think of. Over thirty years, from Microsoft's founding in 1975, the PC revolution changed the world.

The last big leap in the PC revolution was the Internet: Microsoft helped put computers everywhere, and the Internet connected them. Google stands out as the biggest success of the Internet era. We can single out Google's initial public offering (IPO) in August 2004 as the end of the PC revolution. It was the most successful Internet IPO in history. Internet companies went from being risky ventures to investments with solid stocks. Google stock in early 2007 was worth more than $150 billion.

In computers, as in science, the end of a revolution means that what was once revolutionary now becomes normal. The battle is over. PCs won. There will be more advances in PCs, and perhaps something else will come along some day to replace them. But 1975 to 2004—from Microsoft to Google—was the time when the PC revolution took place.

Google's strategic innovation was how to make money from Internet search. In the previous era Microsoft helped computers connect to each other through common software loaded on every machine. The Internet was a new way to connect PCs, but it started out as a public network for U.S. researchers. Nobody owned it. This public character made it hard to make money. The few early Internet giants, like Netscape and Amazon, mostly lost money, although their stock prices sometimes stayed high while investors bet on the future. Then Google turned the most common use of the Internet—free search—into a way of making money.

Did strategic intuition play a role in Google's success? Again, let's look at the details of how it happened to see what we can find out.

The "Google guys" are Sergey Brin and Larry Page. As with Gates's *The Road Ahead* for Microsoft, we have a book that tells us how Google started: *The Google Story* by David Vise, published in 2005.[12] Vise combed through all the public statements about Google and interviewed everyone involved. He tells us what the Google guys did and what they thought at each step of their achievement. Thanks to Vise, we know how Brin and Page came up with their big idea.

Our tale begins at Stanford University in Palo Alto, California, the heart of Silicon Valley. Stanford was an early incubator of advanced engineering companies, starting with Hewlett-Packard (HP). Bill Hewlett and David Packard were students of Stanford professor Frederick Terman. Some date the start of Silicon Valley to HP's founding in 1939. Page and Brin were students of Stanford professor Rajeev Motwani and founded their company in Silicon Valley six decades after Hewlett and Packard founded HP.

Motwani's specialty was data mining. In conventional marketing data mining runs elaborate mathematical algorithms on vast amounts of information on what customers buy in stores. Then you look for patterns to understand the market better. Brin was Motwani's number one graduate student. Together they started a research group on the subject, called MIDAS: MIning Data At Stanford. Page was Motwani's graduate student too, but he was working on something else: the Digital Libraries Project. Everyone expected digital files to replace books to a great degree or even completely, so most big universities like Stanford had some kind of project to work on the transition.

Meanwhile, the Internet era arrived. We can date its birth from Netscape's successful IPO in August 1995. Suddenly an Internet company was worth $3 billion. For their part Motwani and Brin wondered how to apply data mining algorithms to Internet commerce. Page kept working away on the Digital Libraries Project. Page and Brin became best friends and kept in touch with each other's projects.

Four months after the Netscape IPO, DEC released AltaVista, which quickly became the leading search engine of the day. AltaVista downloaded the entire Web onto many powerful computers in order to perform the first full-text search of the Internet. One day Page was browsing AltaVista for his Digital Libraries Project. Vise tells us that Page saw something unusual in AltaVista itself:

> While it returned somewhat better and faster results than the other search engines, Page noticed something else entirely. In addition to a list of Web sites, AltaVista's search results included seemingly obscure information about something called "links".... Instead of focusing on AltaVista's main search results, Page began pondering what could be gleaned from analyzing the links.[13]

The links worked in reverse. AltaVista let you "Find pages that link to your site." These reverse links reminded Page of academic citations. He recalls:

> Citations are important. It turns out, people who win the Nobel Prize have citations from 10,000 different papers. [Many citations] means your work was important, because other people thought it was worth mentioning.[14]

Academic journals and publishing companies rank scholars by how many citations each scholar gets each year. It was the same as counting reverse links in AltaVista. Page realized that reverse links could rank Web sites in the same way academic citations rank scholars. Right away he told Brin.

Here we see that Page had the first flash of insight that led to Google. Reverse links became the first example from history to combine. The second was AltaVista itself. Page went ahead and mimicked Alta Vista's full-text search by downloading the entire Internet onto Stanford's computers. Brin then offered a third element: data mining algorithms from his work with Motwani. Over the next year Page and Brin wrote a program that combined all three elements. The program used data mining algorithms to search all the reverse links on the Internet and rank these links like academic citations.

It was a classic case of strategic intuition. Three examples from history came together in their minds. Page showed presence of mind in switching from the Digital Libraries Project. As Vise reports Page was not studying AltaVista for its links. He was simply searching and then "noticed something else entirely." It changed the direction of his thought and actions, as presence of mind at work.

Page and Brin called their new program PageRank. At that stage they did not even know they had a search engine. Vise notes:

> Brin and Page were persuaded that they had found the path toward a Ph.D. thesis by applying PageRank to the Internet. . . . Page,

Brin, and Motwani all contributed ideas to the evolving project. Motwani said that it would soon become clear that what they had created together was more than just a way to further their academic research. Without intending to, the trio had devised a ranking system for the Internet, and in the process had inadvertently solved one of the core problems of searching for information on the Web. "It wasn't that they sat down and said, 'Let's build the next great search engine.' They were trying to solve interesting problems and stumbled upon some neat ideas," Motwani said.[15]

Note that they "inadvertently" "stumbled upon" their Internet breakthrough. Brin and Page did not set out to build a search engine, but they finally realized that's what they had done. Their presence of mind freed them to switch goals, to go where the new combination led them. They put together a PageRank prototype for Stanford University to use internally. Page's office mate, Sean Anderson, came up with a catchy new name: Google, which they misspelled from "googol," the mathematical name for 10^{100}. Everyone at Stanford loved Google right away. Page and Brin applied for a patent for PageRank. In March 1998 they offered to sell the patent to AltaVista for $1 million.

The offer took place over dinner at a Chinese restaurant in Palo Alto. Representing AltaVista was its designer Paul Flaherty. He listened and took the offer back to his bosses. A few weeks later Flaherty reported back. The answer was "no." Flaherty explained:

> The people who were running engineering weren't very open to outside technology. . . . They had a big "not invented here" attitude.[16]

Such an attitude—"not invented here"—is the opposite of strategic intuition. Instead, you take the attitude "take from everywhere." If you look only internally for elements to combine, you limit your search dramatically. The wider you search externally, the more elements you find to draw on. DEC had another problem too: it was a hardware company about to merge with another hardware company, Compaq. Flaherty saw the potential of Google, but he was a software guy. DEC lacked presence of mind: they were unable to switch goals or at least pursue multiple goals at once.

Also, the big new Internet idea at the time was a portal, not a search engine. A portal gathers content that users pay for, like e-mail, expert advice, news, clothing, books, or consumer products. What little thought DEC gave to AltaVista was right in line with conventional wisdom about portals, where search was only a minor part. In fact the less search the better. While a portal keeps you on its site as long as possible, to navigate through all its different contents, Google was the opposite of a portal: it sent you quickly to other Web sites.[17]

Page and Brin did not give up. They shopped Google around to other search engines, including Excite and Yahoo. Everyone rejected it. David Filo of Yahoo advised them to take a leave of absence from their Ph.D. program and start their own business, because Filo thought no one would buy Google. Then in August 1998 Page and Brin got a break. They met Andy Bechtolsheim, a cofounder of Sun Microsystems, a vice president at Cisco, and an investor in Internet start-ups. Bechtolsheim listened carefully and realized that Page and Brin really did have the best search engine. He asked them how they would make money from Google. They had no idea. Still, Bechtolsheim wrote them a check for $100,000.

The money gave Page and Brin the confidence to take their leave of absence. They spent the money on components to build more computers to make Google even more powerful, on rent for a small house in Menlo Park, and on their first employee, Craig Silverstein, a fellow Stanford Ph.D. student. Bechtolsheim helped them find more investors, who upped the total to $1 million. In June 1999, at the height of the Internet boom, two venture capital firms, Kleiner Perkins and Sequoia Capital, split a further investment of $25 million. Google joined the ranks of hot new Internet start-ups. But as Vise reports:

> It was a heady moment for Google and its founders. Still, the press release and news coverage of the deal, replete with accolades about the search engine and bold statements about the future, failed to answer a central question. The mystery remained: how did Google plan on making money?[18]

As usual the answer came as another example from history. Page and Brin made sure to keep up with what other search engines were doing. Now it paid off:

> One company that caught Brin's attention, for the simple reason that it seemed to be making money by selling ads to accompany search results, was GoTo.com, later renamed Overture Inc. . . . Brin and Page began studying Overture.[19]

Once again it was presence of mind and a flash of insight that showed Page and Brin what their course of action should be. At the time Page and Brin hated advertisements. On other sites advertisers took full advantage of the Internet's visual powers through banner advertisements and pop-ups that mimicked magazine advertisements. By design the advertisements overshadowed the search. To Page and Brin, that was heresy. In contrast, Overture presented advertisements in simple lists, just like its search results. That was it: Overture had Google-like advertisements. That's why Overture made money. Michael Moritz of Sequoia Capital explains:

> To their eternal credit, Larry and Sergey both lighted on what was happening with [Overture's] business model and came to understand pretty rapidly what an attractive business that was.[20]

Page and Brin did not expect or even want Google's money to come from advertisements. But presence of mind left them open to all possibilities, including advertisements. Instead of "not invented here," like DEC, once again it was "take from everywhere" for Page and Brin. They wrote their own version of the Overture program and added it to Google. Advertisers knew that Google had a vastly greater user base than Overture, so they quickly made the switch. And not a moment too soon. It was early 2000. By the end of the year the dot.com bubble burst. It left Google alone at the top of the heap. Just in time they had figured out how to make money.

Page and Brin did not invent AltaVista, academic citations, data mining, and Overture, but they are the ones who combined them, over four years in a series of flashes of insight. The result was success on a scale far beyond the $1 million they thought PageRank was worth when they first tried to sell it to Flaherty. Google became a virtual monopoly in search, as Microsoft monopolized software. Google brought to a close the great revolution, when computers changed from a rare and expensive business machine to an ordinary part of daily life across the entire world.

The companies that began and ended the revolution—Microsoft and Google—were different in many ways. Microsoft sells integrated software applications to companies and individuals, to install on each computer, while Google sells advertisements that appear in free search results to any Internet user. As Google offers more and more free applications to entice more users to search, it looms ahead as Microsoft's biggest potential threat. Just a few years back no one would have ever dreamed of a search engine as a threat to Microsoft. This too is a lesson for strategic innovation: your next major rival can come from anywhere.

The PC revolution started and ended with strategic intuition. Microsoft and Google began as unexpected combinations of examples from history that came together as a series of flashes of insight. Looking back, we see how the period 1975–2004 was a great leap forward—thirty years of revolutionary change that transformed the computer industry and the world around it. But as with Kuhn's scientific revolution, when we study the details of each new bend in the road, we find that each strategist took elements from the past to make a new combination. Revolutionary change is evolutionary change, only faster.

This is precisely the mentality that business innovation calls for. New ideas come from old ones. What is needed is not permanent revolution but permanent evolution, where you constantly search for a better combination. Sometimes your new strategy has a huge and fast effect, and it looks like revolution. Sometimes it has a smaller and slower effect, and it looks like evolution. But the method is the same.

Let's look at two more examples from the same period to see how strategic innovation worked in the years between Microsoft and Google. Our first example is Apple. Steve Jobs took Apple from one of many contenders in small computers to Microsoft's only serious rival in operating software. Our second example is IBM, which recovered from the greatest losses in the history of business to become the industry leader in integrated computer services. In both cases the leaps of strategic innovation were less dramatic than Microsoft's monopoly on software or Google's monopoly on search. But even on that lesser scale, strategic intuition played the key role.

Jobs tells the Apple story himself, in a 1996 film by Robert Cringely about the computer revolution. Cringely interviews Jobs about a visit he made in December 1979 to Xerox's Palo Alto Research Center (PARC). At the time, Apple had the best-selling PC in a very crowded field. After the Altair came out in 1975 other companies used the Intel 8080 chip to make their own PCs, especially IBM, Radio Shack, Commodore, and Apple. Most added screens, which big computers had already used for years. The Apple II was the only one with a color screen and quickly outsold the others. But competition was fierce, and Apple was the smallest company among the leaders.

Jobs had heard about PARC and knew that other companies had gone to see it and came away impressed. He offered Xerox a chance to invest $1 million in Apple, which would pay off royally when Apple did its IPO in a year or two. In return he and his programming team would get special guided tours of PARC. Apple was hard at work on its next machine, the Lisa, and wanted to make sure it was the best in the industry.

In Cringely's film Jobs tells us what he found:

> They showed me really three things. But I was so blinded by the first one I didn't even really see the other two. . . . I was so blinded by the first thing they showed me which was the graphical user interface. I thought it was the best thing I'd ever seen in my life. Now remember it was very flawed, what we saw was incomplete, they'd done a bunch of things wrong. . . . Still though the germ of the idea was there and they'd done it very well and within you know ten minutes it was obvious to me that all computers would work like this some day.[21]

This is the language of a flash of insight. Jobs was "blinded." He "didn't even really see" the other two things. Within ten minutes "it was obvious." Xerox's graphical user interface (GUI) came with a mouse to move the cursor around. The GUI combined in Jobs's mind with Apple's small machines. The Xerox machine was the size of a refrigerator, and Xerox had no plans to make a small one. So Jobs set out to make a small one himself.

The result was the MacIntosh, the first PC with a GUI. It came out in 1984 and cost $2,500. Xerox had come out with its machine three years earlier, in 1981. It cost $16,000, as part of an office suite with multiple machines and a printer for $100,000. Xerox sold very few of them. Jobs hired some of the key PARC staff to help him build the Mac. Xerox could not stop him because the GUI and mouse were both in the public domain. Doug Engelbart had invented them in the 1960s at the Stanford Research Institute with federal money from the Advanced Research Projects Agency. As Jobs predicted all computers adopted the GUI after the Mac.

The title of Cringely's film is *Great Artists Steal*.[22] This is a misquote from T. S. Eliot, the Anglo-American poet who won the Nobel Prize for Literature in 1948. The correct quote is: "Immature poets imitate. Mature poets steal."[23] As a poet, Eliot chose his words very carefully. Jobs did not want to imitate Xerox: if he did that, he'd produce a big machine and sell it for $16,000. Instead, he "stole" certain elements that he saw a way to combine with others. It was selective stealing, not wholesale imitation. Eliot gives us a key distinction that lies at the heart of strategic intuition.

Jobs explains further in another interview, this time for *Wired* magazine in 1996:

> Creativity is just connecting things. When you ask creative people how they did something, they feel a little guilty because they didn't really do it, they just saw something. It seemed obvious to them after a while. That's because they were able to connect experiences they've had and synthesize new things.[24]

Note that for Jobs his Xerox visit was an "experience" he had. He himself did not invent what he saw, but seeing it made it part of his experience, to draw from and "synthesize" with other things on the shelves of his brain. Like Gates, Jobs is a famous visionary, but he has a reputation for creativity too. It makes him "feel a little guilty," because he creates by connecting what he finds. He never invented anything from scratch. Great artists steal: Gates and Jobs alike.

Jobs's flash of insight did not establish a new industry, the way Microsoft was the first software company and Google turned search from a sideshow to the main event. Jobs saw a way to improve a machine he was already working on. The lesson for strategic innovation is simply to take what you find: you don't go looking for a revolutionary idea and you're not disappointed when what you find is less than revolutionary. The Mac gave Apple a burst of success that lasted more than ten years. Jobs went on to the next thing and the next, never inventing anything from scratch but putting together new combinations. Pixar, the iMac, and the iPod stand out among his later successes of this kind.

Our next case, IBM, stands out as an example of how a big company succeeded at strategic innovation. Microsoft, Apple, and Google were all small at the time of their breakthroughs. Strategic innovation seems harder for a big company because there are more people and more layers of management to win over for every new idea. Yet, as big companies today, Microsoft, Apple, and Google still continue their combining ways. For example, Microsoft borrowed the Netscape browser for its own Explorer, Apple borrowed Creative's MP3 player for the iPod, and Google bought YouTube outright for video display.

These more recent innovations of Microsoft, Google, and Apple have changed very little the direction of the company. For IBM strategic innovation took the company in a direction that was not new to the computer industry but was very new to IBM. It was not a great change for the world, but for IBM it was huge. Let's see how this change happened, in order to understand how strategic intuition played out in this different situation.

The head of IBM at the time, Lou Gerstner, tells the story of the company's turnaround in a 2002 book, *Who Says Elephants Can't Dance?*[25] Gerstner had worked as a McKinsey consultant, then moved to American Express, and then became head of RJR Nabisco after its leveraged buyout by Kohlberg Kravis Roberts & Co. After four years the tumult of the buyout—the largest in history—sent Gerstner looking for another job. Meanwhile, IBM was sinking fast. In the 1980s it earned the greatest profits in the history of the world, and in the early 1990s it suffered the greatest losses: $5 billion in 1992 and over $8 billion in 1993. At the end of 1992 a search committee for the IBM board asked Gerstner to take over as CEO.

Gerstner declined, twice. "Given my lack of technical background," he says, "I couldn't conceive of running IBM."[26] At last a member of the committee, Tom Murphy, convinced him:

IBM could be saved. . . . Its problems weren't fundamentally technical in nature. . . . The point Murphy came back to again and again was that the challenge for the next leader would begin with driving the kind of strategic and cultural change that had characterized a lot of what I'd done at American Express and RJR.[27]

Here expert intuition merges into strategic intuition. Gerstner saw elements from his past work to apply to IBM. But at this point he still needed a strategic idea for what IBM should do. He knew the company needed to change but was not yet clear what that change would be.

A partial answer came from a past element. Gerstner recalled his time at American Express:

> I'll never forget the day one of my division managers called and said that he had recently installed an Amdahl computer in a large data center that had historically been 100 percent IBM equipped. He said that his IBM representative had arrived in the morning and told him that IBM was withdrawing all support for his massive data processing center as a result of the Amdahl decision. I was flabbergasted. . . . I placed a call immediately to the office of the chief executive of IBM.[28]

Gerstner succeeded in getting IBM to integrate the Amdahl into the data center. As a former consultant, he knew that the IBM representative had given the wrong answer to the Amdahl request. The right answer was, "We can do it, but it will cost you extra." In the late 1980s and early 1990s all big consulting firms added special technology arms that helped big customers integrate all the different hardware and software products that the computer revolution sent streaming into the market. IBM remained aloof and kept on selling only IBM hardware and only IBM software and servicing only those.

At the time of the Amdahl incident Gerstner had no idea he would leave American Express and one day run IBM. Now at IBM, he found this past example on the shelves of his brain. It was not expert intuition, as he had no expertise in integrating machines and software from different companies. It was an element of strategic intuition, to bring forward as part of his future strategy. And it was a positive element because in the end IBM did make the integration at American Express. The result was a comprehensive package where IBM made money in multiple ways, from some IBM software, some IBM hardware, the work of integrating other hardware and software, and planning and servicing for the whole.

When Gerstner took the IBM job, most Wall Street analysts expected him to break up the company. But he carried forward the Amdahl model as a way of keeping the company together, this time around as key to rather than counter to their normal business practice. The idea was in his mind from his first day on the job,[29] and then he found it already working inside IBM, although on a tiny scale:

> Enter Dennie Welsh. . . . When I arrived at IBM, Dennie was running a wholly owned IBM subsidiary named the Integrated Systems Services Corporation. ISSC was our services and network operations unit in the United States—a promising but minor part of IBM's portfolio. In fact, it wasn't even a stand-alone business in IBM. It was a sub-unit of the sales force.[30]

Dennie Welsh explained his unit to Gerstner. Then and there, Gerstner had the flash of insight he needed to save IBM:

> My mind was afire. Not only was he describing something I'd wanted when I was a customer . . . but this idea meshed exactly with our strategy of integration. . . . I left my session with Dennie both thrilled and depressed (a state of confusion I experienced often in my early days at IBM). I was thrilled that I had discovered a base from which we could build. . . . I was depressed to realize . . . the culture of IBM would fight it.[31]

The past elements that came together in Gerstner's mind were the Amdahl example, Dennie's unit in operation, and Gerstner's experience in strategic and cultural change at previous companies. He had resolution but also saw the rough road ahead.

In the end Gerstner succeeded. IBM's net income went from negative $8.1 billion in 1993 to positive $8.1 billion in 2000. Return on equity over the same period went from negative 35 percent to positive 40 percent. By 2003, the year Gerstner retired, revenues reached $89 billion, the highest in the computer industry. Hardware fell from 49 percent of revenue to 32 percent. Services rose from 20 percent to 48 percent—and switched from maintaining only IBM hardware and software to integrating all kinds of machines and programs.

In this case Gerstner's strategic intuition clearly found him a combination within the grasp of his expert intuition. His expertise in organizational change was one of the past elements he brought forward and combined. Instead of deciding himself which IBM hardware or software products to keep, discard, or build up, he left that part of strategy to the many technical experts within the company. He set himself the task of tearing down the walls that separated the various products from each other and from non-IBM products they found their customers were already using. That he knew how to do. It was a strategy of rearrangement, not invention, along the lines of the Amdahl case and Dennie Welsh's unit. Many consulting firms were already doing integration across products, but IBM had the advantage of vastly superior technical expertise and a storehouse of products to offer as part of the mix.

For big companies strategic innovation likely takes the form of Gerstner's rearrangement, rather than a bold new direction for the whole industry, as with Microsoft or Google in their start-up days. It's an innovation for the company, not for the wider world. But the stakes are the same. In each case you find a Dharma that works for the Karma you face. Gerstner found the right path for IBM. It was not the same path that Gates or the Google guys found, but the method to find the path was the same: past elements came together in their minds as a new combination that showed them the way ahead.

Our four cases in the PC revolution—Microsoft, Google, Apple, and IBM—show that strategic intuition played the key role in giving strategists their main strategic ideas. Yet when we turn to leading ideas in business strategy today, we find entirely different methods. Strategic analysis rules. Strategic intuition is absent. Yet they need not conflict. Strategic analysis and strategic intuition are the two main pieces of the modern puzzle of business strategy. In the rest of this chapter let's see how to fit them together.

Our main source for strategic analysis is Michael Porter's *Competitive Strategy*. Since the book first appeared in 1980, its ideas have dominated the field. Here's how Porter describes it:

> This book presents a comprehensive framework of analytical techniques to help a firm analyze its industry as a whole and predict the industry's future evolution, to understand its competitors and its own position, and to translate this analysis into a competitive strategy for a particular business.[32]

There is no mention of strategic innovation here, but Porter certainly does not exclude it. Innovation might be all or part of the competitive strategy that your analysis leads to. And right away we notice that our strategists from the computer revolution—Gates and Allen, Brin and Page, Jobs, and Gerstner—followed Porter's framework to a great degree, if not explicitly or in the detail that Porter advises. They analyzed their industry as a whole, they predicted the industry's future evolution, and they tried to understand their competitors and their own position. Porter would approve.

But they did not do Porter's last part, where you "translate this analysis into a competitive strategy for a particular business." Their analysis did not lead to their strategic innovations. It is here that Porter misses how strategic ideas really arise. The analysis you do gives you a deep understanding of the situation you face in your industry. It does not give you an idea for what to do about it. Strategic analysis is not the same as strategy formulation, for innovation or any other kind of strategy. Analyzing and strategizing are not the same thing.

Porter says as much in the subtitle of his book: *Techniques for Analyzing Industries and Competitors*. Sure enough, the book is about the analytical parts. He devotes less than half a page to the last part, where you translate analysis into strategy. We find it in Porter's figure below.[33]

Porter gets to formulating strategy only in C2 and C3. Here you compare "feasible strategic alternatives" with your analysis up to

Process for Formulating a Competitive Strategy

A. What Is the Business Doing Now?
  1. Identification: What is the implicit or explicit current strategy?
  2. Implied Assumptions: What assumptions about the company's relative position, strengths and weaknesses, competitors, and industry trends must be made for the current strategy to make sense?

B. What Is Happening in the Environment?
  1. Industry Analysis: What are the key factors for competitive success and the important industry opportunities and threats?
  2. Competitor Analysis: What are the capabilities and limitations of existing and potential competitors, and their probable future moves?
  3. Societal Analysis: What important governmental, social, and political factors will present opportunities or threats?
  4. Strengths and Weaknesses: Given an analysis of industry and competitors, what are the company's strengths and weaknesses relative to present and future competitors?

C. What Should the Business Be Doing?
  1. Tests of Assumptions and Strategy: How do the assumptions embodied in the current strategy compare with the analysis in B above? How does the strategy meet the test in Figure 1-3 (Internal Consistency, Environmental Fit, Resource Fit, Communications and Implementation)
  2. Strategic Alternatives: What are the feasible strategic alternatives given the analysis above? (Is the current strategy one of these?)
  3. Strategic Choice: Which alternative best relates the company's situation to external opportunities and threats?

that point and then you pick the best alternative. This is all he tells us. Nowhere in the book does Porter explain where a feasible strategic alternative comes from. How do you get an idea for what to do? Porter doesn't tell us. Instead he offers some alternatives to consider: a chapter each on *vertical integration, capacity expansion,* and *entry into new business.* But these are hardly the only solutions a business can adopt, and Porter does not give us a specific plan of action or any guidance on how to choose among the various options. He simply does not cover strategy formulation because his subject is strategy analysis.

Yet Porter has made a great contribution to strategy, as Jomini did a century and a half before him. Jomini provided common terms and an understanding of what they meant for the military around the world. He made strategy a military profession. Thanks in large part to Porter, strategy today is a worldwide business profession. Perhaps a million business undergraduates and graduate students over the past twenty-five years have learned about Porter's industry analysis, competitor analysis, and competitive advantage. These terms are now so common that most who use them probably don't know that Porter was their source, just as the military has mostly forgotten that Jomini brought them strategy, tactics, and logistics.

And like Jomini, Porter needs von Clausewitz. Study Jomini and you might conclude that military strategy is simply a matter of choosing an objective and marching your troops to get there. Study Porter and you might think that business strategy is simply a matter of analyzing your industry, your competitors, and your own competitive advantage. Jomini and Porter have done great service in producing basic manuals of their professions, but for making strategy for the uncertain world of the future von Clausewitz leads the way.

And as with Jomini, we can reconcile Porter's work with strategic innovation by placing his analysis before and after strategic intuition. That's what Gates did. Before the Altair his analysis told him that machines were getting smaller and the new Intel chip would play a key role in that. After the Altair his analysis told him that software would become a new industry to serve all the smaller machines. But analysis did not give Gates his strategy—to combine BASIC and the Altair for a monopoly on operating software for mass-market small machines. The strategy itself came from strategic intuition.

In all our cases from the PC revolution our strategists had an ongoing analysis of the situation and then came their flash of insight that brought together selected examples from history as a future course of action. They then assessed that course in light of their new analysis. In most cases they did not have an analysis different from that of many others in the industry. What made them different was the precise examples from history that combined in only their minds and then their resolution to take the action they saw in their minds.

This sequence of analysis–intuition–analysis reconciles Porter's methods with strategic intuition. Yet Porter is an economist, and economics as a discipline has mostly taken a dim view of intuition, in line with the old model of the two-sided brain that places intuition in opposition to analysis. To bridge the gap between economic analysis and strategic intuition, we must overcome this opposition. Yet new research in behavioral economics seems to widen the gap even further, by singling out the economic errors that intuition makes.

The leading figure in behavioral economics is Daniel Kahneman. His 2002 Nobel Prize in Economics cites him "for having integrated insights from psychological research into economic science, especially concerning human judgment and decision-making under uncertainty."[34] Strategic innovation is definitely decision making under uncertainty, so Kahneman's work is certainly relevant. His main subject is "intuitions—thoughts and preferences that come to mind quickly and without much reflection."[35] He published his main findings in a 1982 book, *Judgment Under Uncertainty: Heuristics and Biases.*[36] Heuristics are rules of thumb that people apply automatically in uncertain situations.

Kahneman tells us:

These heuristics are highly economical and usually effective, but they lead to systemic and predictable errors. A better understanding of these heuristics and of the biases to which they lead could improve judgments and decisions in situations of uncertainty.[37]

Note that intuition works by heuristics that are "highly economical and usually effective." So intuition is good. But this is not strategic intuition because Kahneman's work dates from the days of the two-sided brain. In his Nobel lecture Kahneman cites "two generic modes of cognitive function: an intuitive mode, in which judgments and decisions are made automatically and rapidly, and a controlled mode, which is deliberate and slower."[38] Kandel's 2000 Nobel Prize in Neuroscience contradicts that distinction: intelligent memory combines analysis and intuition in a single mode of thought, like the flashes of insight that fueled the PC revolution.

If we take a closer look at Kahneman's work, we find that his heuristic errors might also be errors of expertise. Here is the first study he cites in his 1982 book:

Consider the following example:
The mean IQ of the population of eighth graders in a city is known to be 100. You have selected a random sample of 50 children for a study of educational achievement. The first child tested has an IQ of 150. What do you expect the mean IQ to be for the whole sample?
The correct answer is 101. A surprisingly large number of people believed that the expected IQ for the sample is still 100.[39]

This experiment is now typical in the field of behavioral economics. It gives you a puzzle designed to force an error of judgment. But in this case, does the experiment show an intuitive bias or that the subjects were not very good at statistics? In most professional situations answering 100 when the answer is 101 is a very good guess. In high finance, perhaps, that slight difference might amount to millions of dollars. That's why financial experts need to know statistics. In either case it's a matter of expertise. Our ordinary subjects are not expert enough in statistics to give the right answer. If financial experts make the same mistake, their expert intuition is not good enough to draw on the right statistical formula fast enough.

Kahneman's work and behavioral economics overall seem to show the limits of expert intuition. But those limits do not apply to strategic intuition. The IQ experiment above does not ask the subjects to make a strategic decision. Kahneman knew beforehand the right answer was 101, because a statistical formula says so. This is very different from real-time strategy, where nobody knows what will happen in the future. Strategic innovation is precisely a game of making guesses about the future. Nobody knows the answer beforehand. As a result behavioral economics has yet to design an experiment to test strategic intuition. It is hard to imagine what such an experiment might be. Real-time strategic decisions are simply too complex and uncertain to replicate in an experiment.[40]

Kahneman and behavioral economics enter business strategy in a formal way as subjective probability in pro forma financial statements. Whatever strategy you decide on the pro forma statement projects it forward as revenue, cost, and profit. As a leading textbook in financial accounting tells us, "The preparation of pro forma financial statements requires the analyst to make assumptions about the future. The usefulness of the pro forma financial statements depends on the reasonableness of those assumptions."[41] Assumptions about the future depend on the probability that what you think will come true.

There are three kinds of probability: a priori, where you know the answer, as in Kahneman's IQ example; empirical, based on observed data, as in a survey or poll; and subjective, where

somebody makes a guess. A leading textbook in managerial statistics notes the following:

> The assignment of subjective probabilities to various events is
> usually based on a combination of an individual's past experience,
> personal opinion, and analysis of a particular situation. Subjective
> probability is especially useful in making decisions in situations
> in which the probability of various events cannot be determined
> empirically.[42]

Strategic innovation depends on subjective probability for its
assumptions about the future. Economists further distinguish
between risk, where you know the likelihood of all possible outcomes, and uncertainty, where many outcomes are possible and
we don't know their likelihood:[43] in strategic innovation we don't
know which innovation will work; the future is uncertain, and
our risk projections don't apply. Uncertainty and subjective probability leave us with no formal method for simulating strategic
innovation through finance, economics, or statistics.

Gates and Allen make a bet that software will become a big
business, separate from hardware. No amount of industry analysis or empirical research will be able to tell them beforehand
whether they're right. Brin and Page make a bet that search, not
portals, will win out over the Internet. No method can tell them
beforehand whether they're right. Same with Jobs and the GUI on
small machines and Gerstner for integrated services. Pro forma
financial statements and other kinds of projections are methods
not for determining which bet to make but for expressing your
bet in financial terms.

Tools of finance, economics, and statistics give us no formal
method for making a bet on an uncertain future. Strategic intuition does give us such a method, but in a conservative manner.
All our strategists from the PC revolution combined elements
that worked before but in a new combination to suit a new and
uncertain situation. At the time of your flash of insight there's no

way to prove you're right. That's why you need resolution, von Clausewitz's fourth step.

Although modern economists like Porter leave out strategic innovation and strategic intuition, we find both ideas in a previous era. In the 1940s Joseph Schumpeter of the Austrian School put strategic innovation as the engine of economic success. Through *creative destruction,* innovations kill off old ways and the companies that stick to them. Innovations come from the *personal intuition* and *force* of individual entrepreneurs, either self-employed or at any level in a company, even the "humblest." The innovation itself is a *combination* of what came before, rather than an original invention. It can be a new product or service or a new way of setting up or organizing a business.[44]

Schumpeter's combination of what came before amounts to examples from history. His personal intuition is a flash of insight. His force is resolution. All that's missing from von Clausewitz is presence of mind.

In recent years business writers have rediscovered Schumpeter's ideas: *The Innovator's Dilemma* by Clayton Christensen, *Creative Destruction* by Foster and Kaplan, and *The Strategy Paradox* by Michael Raynor.[45] These books all stress how creative destruction makes it difficult for a company to switch from current success in a declining business to uncertain success in a new business. But these books miss where Schumpeter explains how to find that new business, through strategic intuition. The truer heir to Schumpeter is Amar Bhidé, who asks large numbers of successful entrepreneurs the details of their business history. In *Origin and Evolution of New Businesses* (2000) Bhidé tells us that great artists steal: more than two thirds of his entrepreneurs "replicated or modified an idea encountered through previous employment."[46]

Schumpeter's economic ideas reassure us that modern companies can combine the analytical methods that Porter and his fellow economists advise with the discipline of strategic intuition. In fact, modern practice already does so. For example, a leading textbook in corporate finance tells us that financial forecasts come at the second stage of strategy formulation: the first stage is "creative and largely qualitative."[47] At that first stage successful executives often use strategic intuition without even knowing they are using it. Kahneman warns us about biases in our intuition under uncertainty in that creative stage, but he also praises how well it usually works.

Like the scientific revolution, the PC revolution called for tremendous technical analysis at every stage. Science and business are both hard work to master. But technical analysis alone will lead you in the same direction. For strategic innovation you must change direction. In each of our cases—Microsoft, Google, Apple, and IBM—the idea for that new direction arose through strategic intuition. For any domain of human achievement, whatever the content of the elements to combine, intelligent memory works the same way: a flash of insight, a bend in the road, and on to a new adventure.

8

Mouse, Minister, and Moneylender

The Art of What Works in Social Enterprise

Business has it easy. If strategic intuition changes your goal—like Gerstner's switch from hardware to integration—at least you keep to your overall purpose, which is making money. Same with science, as when Kuhn's flash of insight switched his goal from showing how Aristotle was wrong to showing how Aristotle was right. Kuhn still kept to his overall purpose of advancing scientific knowledge.

In the social sector you don't have the same freedom to modify your goal. Social agencies state a noble mission and funders give them money to carry out the mission. Strategic intuition often changes your goal, and presence of mind means you always stay open to the possibility of changing your goal even if you never end up doing so. Social agencies commit to a goal and stick to it. Does that make them exempt from strategic intuition? The social sector appears to be a Jomini field by nature, where you set a goal and march resolutely to reach it.

For the most part this is certainly true in practice. Kuhn remarks that a natural scientist "concentrates his attention on problems that he has a good reason to believe he will be able to solve," but the social realm defends its choice of problems "chiefly in terms of the social importance of achieving a solution." He asks, "Which group would one expect to solve problems at a more rapid rate?"[1] Of course we have no common measure to calculate whether business and science solve their problems faster than social agencies solve social problems. Yet we do know that in recent years many social agencies have come to admire business and science for their ability to solve problems and have set out to become more businesslike and more scientific as a way to better results.

As we saw in previous chapters strategic intuition is both businesslike and scientific in its method of finding strategic ideas. In this chapter we study three cases where strategic intuition solved major social problems: how American women won the right to vote, how Martin Luther King led the civil rights movement, and how Muhammad Yunus won the Nobel Peace Prize in 2006 for starting the microcredit movement. We also learn about a practical tool, the *what-works matrix* from General Electric (GE), that social agencies can use to integrate strategic intuition into their normal operations.

Yet the biggest obstacle to social agencies adopting strategic intuition is the spread of popular Jomini methods that seem businesslike and scientific. We cannot underestimate the Jomini problem. We take a close look at two of these methods: conventional strategic planning and theories of change. Our three major cases of strategic intuition in action help us understand how the what-works matrix of strategic intuition is a closer match for how social achievements actually happen than these two Jomini tools. Strategic intuition, not strategic planning or theories of change, can help the social sector become more businesslike and scientific.

Some of this recent interest in borrowing from business and science to solve social problems comes from successful business executives with a science background entering the social sector—Bill Gates is only the most famous of many. Google recently entered too, with Google.org and the Google Foundation. But the main attraction of business and science comes from the obvious success of these sectors in the past few decades. Perhaps with similar methods social programs can achieve similar results.

This heightened interest in results—rather than simply contributing to a worthy cause—comes from greater competition within the social sector. There are so many social agencies now—the Internal Revenue Service recognizes 1.5 million nonprofit organizations—that they end up competing for funding. If your agency can show results, you might win the competition. If you can't show results, critics attack your nonprofit status and demand that the money go into the regular tax system to fund government programs instead. More and more, even government agencies in the social sector need to show results to keep their funding.

The businesslike drive for results has turned social agencies into social enterprises: you try to be enterprising in everything you do. For example, when your program delivers food to poor people, social enterprise asks you how to do it better, faster, and cheaper, including better ways to organize and fund your agency. Every aspect of social enterprise calls for some kind of business skill. Strategy is a core business skill, and sure enough social agencies have taken to strategy as a way to become more businesslike. Through his Center for Effective Philanthropy,[2] Michael Porter has translated his methods of strategic analysis for the social sector. Beyond analysis, for actual strategy formulation, social enterprise has adopted classical strategic planning as standard practice around the world. Here Jomini reigns supreme.

Let's look at a popular guide to strategic planning for nonprofit agencies, the Wilder Foundation's *Strategic Planning Workbook for Nonprofit Organizations* by Bryan Barry. We learn that "strategic planning is developing a shared vision of your nonprofit's future, then determining the best way for that vision to occur." This is exactly Jomini's march from A to B. Sure enough, Figure 1 of the *Strategic Planning Workbook* shows a circle for the *present* and a straight-line arrow to a circle for the *desired future*.[3] Yet *Strategic Planning Workbook* adds:

> You cannot develop a perfect strategic plan. The world changes too quickly. Most organizations use their strategic planning to get general agreement on where their organization should be headed, along with the major steps or paths to get there. The plan serves as

an orienting vision which helps people and programs keep moving toward agreed-upon goals. As people learn which strategies work (and which do not) and where the most fruitful opportunities lie, they adjust their goals and path accordingly. . . . The design gets clearer and better after you begin shaping your organization's future and determining what's possible. Therefore, many organizations formally update their strategic plan regularly (every one to three years) and make more frequent adjustments in strategy as they learn what works.[4]

So we end up with Jomini planning, plus the ability to adjust your *goals and path* as your strategy proceeds, as you *learn what works*. We can call this *flexible Jomini*. The flexible part is good, but we still have a basic problem that starts in step 1, your original shared vision of your nonprofit's future. Here's what *Strategic Planning Workbook* tells us: "How does your organization determine the best course for the future? One key is finding the fit among three forces—your organization's mission, outside opportunities, and your organization's capabilities."[5] We get no guidance on how to establish a mission in the first place. As for outside opportunities you find them through an analysis of the needs of customers and other stakeholders, of competitors and allies, and of social, economic, political, and technological forces. For your organization's capabilities, these are "the resources or competence that your nonprofit has or could develop." We see then that *Strategic Planning Workbook* helps us find our strategy by combining our mission and strategic analysis in the Porter tradition. And we must do this in a participatory way, so that we get a general agreement on the vision and agreed-upon goals.

From the view of strategic intuition there is one fatal flaw: *learn what works* comes at the end, not the beginning. *Strategic Planning Workbook* tells you to start with your mission and then you combine that mission with strategic analysis to find your vision. Then you set your goals and path and periodically adjust your goals and path when you learn what works. In strategic intuition *what works* animates all these steps, starting with your original mission. For von Clausewitz what works equals examples from history. That's where strategy starts.

Here we come back to the key difference between business and social programs. For nonprofit organizations their mission starts with someone's belief in what's right. For public agencies their mission comes from what people who rule the government believe is right. How can we ignore what's right and decide our mission instead by what works? That could mean giving up what's right. Don't great leaders see the future first and then motivate their followers to reach it?

Gates and Allen, Brin and Page, Jobs and Gerstner won a reputation as visionaries in business, but we saw that they actually succeeded by strategic intuition. Their visions of the future came by combining what works. As it turns out, our social examples succeeded in the same way. Let's turn to these social examples now, to see how our visionaries in women's suffrage, civil rights, and microfinance figured out what to do. Did they follow *Strategic Planning Workbook* or strategic intuition?

Our first case, American women's fight for the right to vote, starts with Susan B. Anthony. She is the most famous woman in American history, thanks to her tireless pursuit of women's suffrage. For fifty-four years, from 1852, she carried the flame without pause. In 1906, on her eighty-sixth birthday, she gave her most famous speech, "Failure Is Impossible," in Washington, D.C. Four weeks later she died.

Fourteen years after that, in 1920, women won the right to vote. Anthony said, "Failure is impossible," and she certainly succeeded in keeping the movement alive. She deserves her place in history. But she did not succeed in winning the right to vote. Were the next fourteen years simply a matter of her followers tirelessly carrying out her vision through to the final success, as *Strategic Planning Workbook* might suggest?

Enter Carrie Chapman Catt. She inherited Anthony's organization, NAWSA—the National American Women's Suffrage

Association. Catt kept up Anthony's two principal methods: (1) delegations of prominent women asking individual legislators in the states and in Washington to give women the right to vote and (2) organizing large conventions where women come together to hear speakers on women's suffrage. Unfortunately it wasn't working. NAWSA had succeeded only in a few states, and at that rate all women would get the right to vote only by the year 2000.

Enter Alice Paul. After degrees from Swarthmore and the University of Pennsylvania, she won a fellowship to study and practice social work in England in 1907. She showed no interest in women's suffrage and certainly had no vision for how to achieve it. Yet in England Paul put together examples from history that won American women the right to vote.

There in England she discovered Emmeline Pankhurst. England had its own version of NAWSA, the National Union of Women's Suffrage Societies (NUWSS). In 1903, at the age of forty-five, Pankhurst broke away from NUWSS to found another organization, the Women's Social and Political Union. She adapted tactics from the British labor movement, such as illegal picketing, dramatic marches, and hunger strikes in jail. Pankhurst even put women on horses at the head of her parades. Her lovely daughter Christabel became the poster girl for the movement as well as a fiery leader in her own right. And they started succeeding: outrage in the press over the arrest and force-feeding of hunger strikers led to politicians endorsing the cause, including the future prime ministers David Lloyd George and Winston Churchill.[6]

Paul joined in. She marched, got arrested, went on a hunger strike, and suffered force-feeding. In a London police station Paul met Lucy Burns, a fellow American her age. The police put the ladies in the station billiard room, instead of mixing them in with ordinary criminals. Paul and Burns sat side by side on the billiard table, plotting their American campaign. In 1910 Paul returned to America with not only the elements of a successful campaign but also a key ally.

It was Alice Paul, not Carrie Catt, who led the final push for women's suffrage. Paul went ahead on her own, first by heading a sleepy NAWSA committee that she turned into a version of Pankhurst's English organization. Now came the American era of dramatic marches, picketing, arrests, and hunger strikes in prison. Paul put her version of Christabel Pankhurst on a horse at the head of her parades: Inez Milholland Boissevain, a lawyer with the looks of a movie star. Paul's biggest parade with Boissevain at the head was at Woodrow Wilson's 1912 inauguration. Crowds of men attacked the marchers. Just like in England outrage led to progress. Six weeks later both houses of Congress introduced bipartisan legislation for women's suffrage. Paul made more progress in two years than Anthony had made in fifty years.

Catt reacted by denying Paul further use of NAWSA, so Paul formed her own National Woman's Party. More and more states granted women the right to vote. In Washington, D.C., the federal suffrage amendment stalled because Woodrow Wilson opposed it. His Democratic Party controlled both houses of Congress. So in 1917 Paul took up Pankhurst's most powerful weapon. It was time to go to jail. At first Paul stayed behind the scenes while Burns led the way. Women picketed the White House. Burns was the first one arrested. Dozens more followed. After four months of arrests, Paul decided to go herself.

Then, following the Pankhurst model again the women went on a hunger strike. Sure enough, the jailers force-fed them. Paul herself was physically frail—a friend described her as "almost mouselike"[7]—and force-feeding in England had almost killed her. She started failing fast. Woodrow Wilson took note. Would history remember him as the great peacemaker who founded the League of Nations or the tyrant who killed Alice Paul?

Wilson sent an emissary, David Lawrence, to negotiate a compromise with Paul. She refused. A few days later the prison released Paul and all the others. That was the end of November, 1917. The next week the House of Representatives schedule a vote on the amendment for a few weeks later, January 10, 1918. On

January 9 President Wilson declared his support for women's suffrage. That was it: the amendment went on to pass in the House, Senate, and eventually all the states.[8] The mouse, not Catt, had won the day.

Paul found her winning strategy not from conventional strategic planning but as a flash of insight on a billiard table in England. She did not start out with a mission to win women the right to vote. But she did have a more general goal of improving women's welfare, and at the time social work seemed a useful way to do that. She switched from social work as a means to that end only when she saw a way to win at women's suffrage instead, when Emmeline Pankhurst and Lucy Burns came together in her mind there in the London police station.

What works came into play at the start of Paul's strategy, not at the end as a way to adjust the strategy. For women's suffrage that made all the difference. Catt's resistance to changing her own strategic plan reflects a common problem in the social sector. Her overall mission got mixed up with a particular organization—NAWSA—which in turn had its own traditional strategy. For Catt to switch she had to admit that her current path was not working. This is very hard for anyone to do, let alone a respected leader with plenty of followers already. Yet presence of mind demands it, or you risk missing the bend in the road that leads to greater success.

Our next example is Martin Luther King. He stands out both for his great contribution to civil rights and as an inspiration for all kinds of achievement. Like Susan B. Anthony, he had a dream and did everything he could to make the dream come true. It even cost him his life. We might jump to the conclusion that King laid out a vision first and then a plan of action to realize it. He declared his mission in a famous speech, "I Have a Dream," to an audience of a quarter million at the March on Washington. His goal was a Civil Rights Act. His speech launched a massive movement to make that vision come true.

Or did it?

President John F. Kennedy introduced the Civil Rights Act to Congress in June 1963. King's speech came two months later, in August. Kennedy's assassination in November sealed the act's passage. By this timeline King's great speech was a pep talk to clear the final hurdle, not a spark to ignite the whole movement. His speech laid out his vision, but at the end—not the start—of the civil rights campaign.

It was not King's vision that set him above other civil rights leaders. The vision King had at the start of the movement was no different from that of countless other black Americans. They all dreamed of an America without segregation or prejudice. His most famous predecessor was Frederick Douglass, way back in Susan B. Anthony's time. Douglass had the same dream as King. It was hardly Douglass's fault that he did not succeed, just as it was not Anthony's fault that she died before women won the right to vote. But did King simply follow in Douglass's footsteps and the country finally accepted the idea, or did King do something different, the way Alice Paul did something different from Anthony?

What made King different was not his dream. His talent as a speaker helped a great deal, but that was not the key to his success either. Great speeches can move people, but you want the people to move in the right direction. And the *right* direction is not simply the morally right thing to do. It has to be what works.

Let's go back to the start of the great push in the civil rights era, starting with *Brown v. Board of Education of Topeka*, Kansas, in 1954, when the Supreme Court declared segregation illegal in the nation's schools. Ten years later came the Civil Rights Act. What happened over those ten years?[9]

The *Brown* decision was a great victory for the NAACP—the National Association for the Advancement of Colored People. Lawyers did it, with Thurgood Marshall in the lead. The NAACP was founded in 1909, and *Brown* was its first big breakthrough. From 1954 on, branches of the NAACP throughout the country, especially the South, started working to desegregate schools to comply with the *Brown* decision. In each city or town you filed a lawsuit to make the local school district conform to *Brown*. Unfortunately that strategy did not work. By 1960 fewer that 1 percent of black children in the South went to integrated schools. Some districts simply disbanded their schools rather than let blacks in. Topeka itself, the district cited in the *Brown* decision, complied with the court's full standards of desegregation only in 1998.

Even before *Brown* there was a small group of NAACP members who wanted to try something other than lawsuits. They wanted to take Mahatma Gandhi's example from India and start a campaign of nonviolent civil disobedience. Bayard Rustin studied Gandhi's techniques and practiced them over the years but without any lasting effect. Ella Baker was the highest ranking NAACP woman, as director of local branches, and she wanted the NAACP to try nonviolent civil disobedience. But she left the NAACP in 1946, frustrated by the bureaucracy and lack of action. Occasionally she worked as a trainer in nonviolent techniques at the Highlander School in Tennessee. She tried to practice them too, but the men argued against women putting themselves in danger. Rustin and others got beat up more than once.

When the NAACP won *Brown* everyone turned to schools. Baker, Rustin, and a wealthy lawyer, Stanley Levison, founded an organization together, In Friendship, to raise money for school desegregation lawsuits in New York City. *Brown* was such a breakthrough that even the advocates of civil disobedience switched to follow the path of lawsuits to desegregate schools.

Then, in March 1955 Rosa Parks, an active NAACP member in Montgomery, Alabama, helped E. D. Nixon, the local head of the NAACP, try a bus boycott. The idea came from Jackie Robinson, the first black baseball player in the major leagues, who refused to move to the back of an army bus while he was a soldier, in 1944. Robinson won his court martial case. A few years later Rustin followed in Robinson's footsteps by trying to ride a segregated interstate bus. The action led nowhere. Now Nixon wanted to try again. He wanted someone to get arrested for refusing to move to the back of a bus, so he could lead a boycott of the entire Montgomery bus system.

Nixon's first candidate for the boycott was Claudette Colvin, a fifteen-year-old member of the NAACP's local youth council. She went ahead and got arrested. Then Nixon learned that Colvin was pregnant by a much older, married man. Nixon knew that the scandal would kill the boycott. So he called it off. Then in June, Rosa Parks attended one of Ella Baker's Highlander workshops. In December, Parks refused to move to the back of the bus. It was a spontaneous act, but in doing so she knew she was Nixon's next candidate. He came to jail and bailed her out. So began the Montgomery bus boycott.

At that time the NAACP as a whole still thought that lawsuits to desegregate schools were the best way to achieve their vision of an integrated America. Rustin and Baker were part of a minority who wanted to bring to America Gandhi's nonviolent methods, but they had a hard time getting started, so they switched to *Brown* like everyone else. Nixon, Parks, and Claudette Colvin were an even smaller minority who wanted to try a boycott. Nobody knew which of these methods—or any other—would work.

The black community of Montgomery rallied to Rosa Parks's defense. They had nowhere to meet, so black ministers offered their churches. Nixon helped them form a Montgomery Improvement Association to run the boycott and proposed Martin Luther King Jr., the youngest of the ministers, to serve as president.

King hesitated at first. There had been a few ministers active in civil rights, but as a whole they stayed out of politics. King was only twenty-six, with a Ph.D. in theology from Boston University. He knew nothing about nonviolent civil disobedience or boycotts, and he had no plans—no vision of the future—to get involved in any of it. His vision was to follow in his father's footsteps: Martin Luther King Sr. was a prominent minister in Atlanta. King Sr. did join the NAACP and become head of the Atlanta division, so King Jr. joined Montgomery's. Still, the NAACP in those days did not break the law. Civil disobedience meant going to jail, which for black men in the South was a mark of doom.

The Montgomery bus boycott landed on King Jr.'s doorstep. His congregation, elder ministers, and the wider community asked him to take the lead. It is to the great credit of young Dr. King that in the end he said yes. He was already a good speaker, and over the year of the boycott he became a great one. The content of his speeches switched from the details of the boycott to examples from history he knew very well, such as the Bible and the great documents of American history, especially the Constitution, Declaration of Independence, and Lincoln's Gettysburg Address.

But still King knew nothing about civil disobedience. No one else in Montgomery did either. So Bayard Rustin arrived from New York. He quickly taught them the basics. For example, here's how to get arrested: instead of waiting for the police to come to you, as soon as you know the warrant is out you call the police station and schedule a time to turn yourself in. Then you call your followers and the press to show up. The arrest turns into a parade, well covered in newspapers. With photographers around the police do not even think of roughing you up.

Back in New York, Baker and Levison turned the mission of In Friendship from *Brown* to Montgomery. They raised money to help the boycott. After a year, in December 1956, the boycott succeeded. The Supreme Court ruled against the bus company. Right away, King and other ministers across the South wanted to replicate the Montgomery success, but it was not obvious how to do it.

The answer came that same December, as a flash of insight to Rustin, Baker, and Levison at the same time, in Levison's kitchen on the Upper West Side of Manhattan. They were working on something else: a fund-raising concert with Harry Belafonte. They put three elements together from their pasts: techniques of civil disobedience from Rustin, overseeing NAACP branches from Baker, and raising money from Levison. A fourth element was the successful bus boycott. A fifth element was King as leader. Rustin, Baker, and Levison put the pieces together and wrote up working papers for a new organization to repeat the boycott in other cities.

And so was born the SCLC—the Southern Christian Leadership Conference—in 1957. In 1954, at the *Brown* victory, no one predicted that in just three years ministers would lead a campaign of civil disobedience across the South—let alone a successful one. King's starting vision was to be a prominent minister and an NAACP member, like his father. Even through the bus boycott, that was still a realistic vision for his future because nobody knew if the boycott would work. When it did work King changed his vision for his future to something very different: the leader of a movement of nonviolent civil disobedience across the South. Just a year before no one could have predicted he would play that role, least of all King himself.

Meanwhile, trouble with repeating the *Brown* success for schools led the NAACP to call for explicit federal legislation to make segregation illegal—a Civil Rights Act. The first activity of the new SCLC was to join the NAACP in a prayer meeting in Washington, D.C., to announce this new goal. The new act was based on one from 1875, which the Supreme Court voided in 1883. So a Civil Rights Act was not a new idea, but it was a new goal for the modern civil rights movement. It was not part of anyone's starting vision in 1954.

In its first year the SCLC succeeded with forty-two boycotts across the South. In most cases the bus company gave in right away, figuring it could not win. Soon buses were integrated but nothing else. What next?

There was no other success to take to scale, so the SCLC decided on a voter registration campaign. If blacks voted more, they could elect local officials to overturn local segregation laws and practices. It makes sense in theory, but it's not what works. The NAACP had the same idea as the SCLC, and the two competed locally to register voters. Yet neither organization based their theory on a new combination of what worked in the past. Sure enough, neither campaign succeeded.

After a year Baker proposed that the SCLC give up the voter campaign. Instead, she wanted to replicate the Nashville SCLC, where a divinity student, James Lawson, ran nonviolent civil disobedience workshops at Vanderbilt University. The Nashville SCLC was the strongest formal nonviolent program in the country. Baker wanted to send teams from every SCLC chapter to Lawson's workshop, and she wanted the SCLC to cut down its administrative costs and hire a minister full-time to help her. Also, she wanted King to move to Atlanta to demonstrate his commitment to the new program.

It took her a year, but the SCLC agreed to all her proposals. It wasn't easy being a woman at NAACP headquarters in the 1940s, and it wasn't easy being a woman in the SCLC in the 1950s. But Baker kept at it and finally won out.

And then she switched. Her goal changed again because something else worked.

On January 31, 1960, Montgomery gave King a farewell celebration for his move to SCLC headquarters in Atlanta. The next day, February 1, four black college students in Greensboro, North Carolina, sat down at a white lunch counter in Woolworth's. The four had no training in civil disobedience and had no contact with any civil rights organization. Woolworth's closed for the day to get rid of them. The next day more students joined them and then more through the week, white and black alike. The press and TV showed up.

The sit-ins spread to other lunch counters in Greensboro and then to other cities. The first arrests came on February 12 in Raleigh, North Carolina, where forty-two students went to jail. By the end of the month there were sit-ins in thirty cities and seven states. Every success led to more students joining the next sit-in somewhere else.

Ella Baker swung into action. All through February she telephoned her contacts around the South to spread the word and help the students organize their sit-ins. And during that first month she had a flash of insight: a new organization to replicate sit-ins, just as the SCLC replicated the Montgomery bus boycott. Baker used SCLC funds to host a meeting of students from all the new protests over spring break in April at her alma mater of Shaw College in Raleigh. King and Baker signed the invitation letter together. The letter did not mention a new organization: the purpose of the meeting was to "chart new goals and achieve a more unified sense of direction for training and action in Nonviolent Resistance."

During the meeting Baker counseled the students to form their own group. Leaders from the NAACP, the SCLC, and the third leading civil rights organization, CORE—the Congress for Racial Equality—urged the students to form a youth wing under them. The students listened to Baker. And so began SNCC—the Student Nonviolent Coordinating Committee. They opened an office in Atlanta. Baker quit the SCLC and moved to SNCC to help out.

Now came the great wave of civil disobedience that culminated with King's great speech and the Civil Rights Act. As SNCC grew King and the SCLC adopted sit-ins too and courted younger members. The jails filled with high school and college students, who had no fear of losing their jobs. The younger generation filled the ranks for this last great push. And at the March on Washington John Lewis, the head of the SCLC, was the speaker right before King's "I Have a Dream."

In the end we see that many people had the same dream as King, but that's not what made for success. You need a strategy. King's strategy came from a series of different opportunities that no one foresaw. As with NAWSA and women's suffrage many NAACP leaders did not like the change of goal from desegregating schools. As of 1954, when *Brown* succeeded, no one could foresee that droves of young people going to jail would finally win the day. That's because no one could foresee the success of the Montgomery bus boycott or the Greensboro sit-in. It was not a preconceived vision or a plan that guided King and Baker. Instead, they followed what worked at every step of the way.

Our last example switches fields from civil rights—for women or black Americans—to a bank for poor people in Bangladesh. Here we can see how business skills of many kinds apply directly to a social cause. In starting and operating Grameen Bank, Muhammad Yunus used many of the techniques common among social agencies today. But for his most crucial step—where his strategy came from—which specific tool did he use: *Strategic Planning Workbook* or strategic intuition?

The citation for Yunus's Nobel Peace Prize offers this view:

> Muhammad Yunus has shown himself to be a leader who has managed to translate visions into practical action for the benefit of millions of people, not only in Bangladesh, but also in many other countries. Loans to poor people without any financial security had appeared to be an impossible idea. From modest beginnings three decades ago, Yunus has, first and foremost through Grameen Bank, developed micro-credit into an ever more important instrument in the struggle against poverty. Grameen Bank has been a source of ideas and models for the many institutions in the field of micro-credit that have sprung up around the world.[10]

Here we see that Yunus managed to translate visions into practical action, for something that appeared to be an impossible idea. This is clearly *Strategic Planning Workbook*'s idea: you base your vision on an ambitious idea and then turn your vision into reality. The Grameen Bank Web site gives a similar view:

> The origin of Grameen Bank can be traced back to 1976 when Professor Muhammad Yunus, Head of the Rural Economics Program at the University of Chittagong, launched an action research project to examine the possibility of designing a credit delivery system to provide banking services targeted at the rural poor.[11]

Again we see that Yunus starts with an idea—a vision—and designs a project to test it. But our study of strategic intuition leads us to ask a previous question: How did Yunus get the vision in the first place? We find the answer in Yunus's autobiography, *Banker to the Poor*, and through interviews in two Grameen Bank histories, *The Price of a Dream* by David Bornstein, and *Give Us Credit* by Alex Counts.[12] In these books we find that, as in our previous cases, Yunus did not start out with a vision for microcredit. That vision arose as a series of flashes of insight, based each time on what worked.

Yunus began his career with a very different vision: the green revolution. In the 1970s advances in crop science brought much higher yields to Asian farmers. With enough water, the right techniques, and new hybrid seeds, poor countries could grow much more food than before. As a green revolution economist, Yunus completed his doctorate in the United States and returned to Bangladesh, first as an economist at the National Planning Commission and then as a professor at Chittagong University. Every day he drove to campus:

> Along the way I drove through the village of Jobra. . . . I noticed barren fields next to the village and asked a colleague, H. I. Latifee, why they were not being cultivated for a winter crop. . . . It turned out that there was no water for irrigation.[13]

Yunus had an economic research grant from the Ford Foundation, so he switched the grant to pay his students to organize a cooperative in the village. The cooperative drilled a well and bought, installed, and maintained a motor pump for it. Yunus took a personal loan too, from the campus branch of the Janata Bank. He won the Bangladesh President's Award for his efforts.

So far everything Yunus did was right in line with the green revolution. Yet he was not satisfied. The farmers repaid only two-thirds of the money to him, even though the harvest was good. He noticed something else as well, "a problem I had not focused on before." Landless women worked on the harvest for a pittance. The green revolution was passing them by.

So Yunus asked Latifee to lead him through the village because Latifee "knew most of the families and had a natural talent for making villagers feel at ease." One day they stopped at a destitute household where a woman named Sufiya Begum was making a bamboo stool. They asked her how much she paid for the bamboo, the time it took to make a stool, and the price she sold the stool for. Yunus computed the profit:

> Sufiya Begum earned two cents a day. It was this knowledge that shocked me. In my university courses, I theorized about sums in the millions of dollars, but here before my eyes the problems of life and death were posed in terms of pennies.[14]

If Sufiya Begum bought her bamboo in bulk, for twenty-two cents, she could bypass the trader and make more profit. There were moneylenders in the village, so why not borrow the money from them? But she explained that these moneylenders charged too much. She had one neighbor who was paying 10 percent per day.

In a flash of insight Yunus put together the first two elements of Grameen Bank: a village moneylender and a poor woman with a tiny business. Sufiya Begum simply needed someone to offer a loan with a better rate. Yunus would find that someone to do it. But as von Clausewitz tells us, "Everything in strategy is simple, but that does not mean that it is easy."[15] Sufiya Begum was hardly the only one who needed the money. A quick survey of the village turned up forty-two women like her. Together they borrowed twenty-seven dollars at any one time. Yunus recalls:

> "My God, my God. All this misery in all these families all for the lack of twenty-seven dollars!" I exclaimed. . . . No formal financial structure was available to cater to the credit needs of the poor. This credit market, by default . . . , had been taken over by the local moneylenders.[16]

Here came the third element: a formal financial structure similar to the local Janata Bank. Yet Yunus did not yet think about starting a bank. He was wondering how to get one to help the women and, in the meantime, lent the women twenty-seven dollars of his own money. To his great surprise the women paid it back. This was another element of Grameen Bank: a group of women repaid their loans without collateral. Yet Yunus was still not sure what to do about this. As Bornstein tells it, "'I didn't know what I was doing,' Yunus recalled. 'I certainly had no intention of starting a bank.'"[17] Yunus went to the Janata Bank again and asked for another loan. The manager turned him down because the branch only offered savings accounts. The first loan for the irrigation pump had been a personal favor. Yet Yunus did not want to keep funding the women himself. Bornstein reports:

> 'This was not a solution,' he said. 'Every time they needed money they couldn't come to me.' . . . Yunus decided to pay another visit to the manager of the Janata Bank. He had an idea.[18]

Here is the final flash of insight that put Grameen Bank together. Yunus wanted the bank to make tiny loans directly to the women— ten takas each in Bangladesh currency—instead of lending him the money to lend on to them. Bornstein continues:

> "Ten taka loans?" the manager exclaimed. "That's not even worth the paperwork they have to fill out . . . we can't give loans to poor people. . . . They don't have any collateral." . . . Yunus explained that the villagers were repaying his loans. Why wouldn't they repay the bank's loans?[19]

The local branch manager said no, but the regional manager said yes. Yunus ran the project out of Janata Bank, and as the project grew larger he spun it off as Grameen Bank. The women continued to pay back their loans. The Grameen Bank Web site tells the rest of the story:

> The action research demonstrated its strength in Jobra (a village adjacent to Chittagong University) and some of the neighboring

villages during 1976–1979. With the sponsorship of the central bank of the country and support of the nationalized commercial banks, the project was extended to Tangail district (a district north of Dhaka, the capital city of Bangladesh) in 1979. With the success in Tangail, the project was extended to several other districts in the country. In October 1983, the Grameen Bank Project was transformed into an independent bank by government legislation. Today Grameen Bank is owned by the rural poor whom it serves. Borrowers of the Bank own 90% of its shares, while the remaining 10% is owned by the government.[20]

We see from the details of how Grameen Bank started that Yunus did not first set out a vision and then make a plan to make it come true. Examples from history gave Yunus his vision for Grameen Bank, and this vision changed his plans dramatically. He showed great presence of mind when he toured Jobra village with Latifee and found Sufiya Begum. He expected the unexpected, just like von Clausewitz advises. Yunus entered the village as a green revolution economist and left as a moneylender to the poor.

And yet Yunus's most basic mission, to fight poverty in Bangladesh, never changed. He just found a way to succeed at it. This means that social agencies do not have to change their missions to follow his example, if they keep the mission general enough to embrace many possible paths. The danger is picking a narrow mission before strategic intuition shows you a way to get there. And that does not mean you wait around for inspiration to strike you. Yunus worked hard on his original path of the green revolution. He only switched when he hit upon something better.

In these three cases—women's suffrage, civil rights, and microcredit—success came about without any formal strategic method. Strategic intuition came about as a habit of mind among the leaders, not as a technique for an organization to apply. Do we just abandon all formal methods, like *Strategic Planning Workbook*'s strategic planning? That's asking a lot for social agencies and funders alike.

Yet we do have a way for social agencies to apply strategic intuition as a formal method. We call it the *what-works matrix*, adapted from GE in the late 1990s. Agencies can use the matrix throughout their organizations at every step in strategic planning. It leads you through the early steps of the scientific method as Roger Bacon first described it. That is, first you look for elements that work. It is a formal way to apply the four steps of von Clausewitz to planning of any kind.

We contrast the matrix with a Jomini version of the scientific method that has grown popular in recent years among many social agencies. One such agency is the Bill & Melinda Gates Foundation, which since its founding in the late 1990s has become the world's biggest private philanthropy. What the biggest foundations do has a ripple effect throughout the whole philanthropic sector. So what the Gates Foundation does can tell us much about practice in the overall social sector.

As with most ambitious programs in social enterprise it will take many years to know the outcome of what the Gates Foundation has funded. On their Web site we find the section What We're Learning, which offers progress reports but no final results as yet. So let's look at their methods instead. Elsewhere on the Gates Foundation Web site, under Guiding Principles, we find the following method of strategy: "We identify a specific point of intervention and apply our efforts against a theory of change."[21] Most big foundations these days use this same term, *theory of change*, to some degree.[22] A World Economic Forum report of 2003 on "Benchmarking Philanthropy" notes that nonprofit organizations and funders alike tend to agree on the following version of the idea:[23]

Inputs → Activities → Outputs → Outcomes = Quantitative
Results

This is a theory of change because you hypothesize that your *inputs* will lead to the *outcomes* you want. You decide which cause will have which effect and then attempt to put a cause into action in order to attain its predicted result. Then you measure the actual outcomes to see if your hypothesis came true. Theory of change starts with *Strategic Planning Workbook*'s Jomini march from point A to point B—from where you are now to your desired outcomes. Then theory of change adds social science research to see how close you came to point B.

Theory of change in its current form dates back to Carol Weiss's *Evaluation Research* of 1972. This book became the leading guide for evaluating social programs, first in the United States and later around the world. As social agencies and funders professionalized in the 1990s, Weiss helped them do it. In the second edition of the book, from 1998, we find these key definitions:

> Theories of change: The assumptions that link a program's inputs and activities to the attainment of desired ends; it includes both implementation theory and program theory.
>
> Program theory: Assumptions about the chain of interventions and participant responses that lead to program outcomes.
>
> Implementation theory: The theory that if activities are conducted as planned, with sufficient quality, intensity, and fidelity to plan, they will attain desired results.[24]

Elsewhere in the book Weiss tells us that a theory of change is:

> a set of hypotheses upon which people build their program plans. . . . Scientific generalizations are built up by developing hypotheses and then submitting them to successive tests in an effort to disprove them or find the limits of their applicability.[25]

Now we recognize what theory of change is really about. It's an attempt to apply the scientific method to social enterprise. Unfortunately, it's the wrong scientific method. It's the experimental method you learned in grade school, not the method of scientific achievement as Bacon and Kuhn explained it. In an experiment scientists do want desired results, but after the experiment is over they are delighted to apply their results to some other end they did not set out to achieve in that experiment. And they spend a tremendous amount of effort to find a hypothesis worth testing. The experimental method follows.

The real scientific method is strategic intuition, where you first study the laboratories of other scientists and follow the trail of what works. It leads to unforeseen bends in the road—you expect the unexpected and go where success can take you. As social agencies have become more scientific in measuring results, they have applied the wrong version of the scientific method to their work. Alice Paul, Martin Luther King, and Muhammad Yunus did not start out with a theory of change and then measure how it worked. They combined what worked to come up with their theory of change to begin with.

As Bill Gates moved to the social sector it seems he left behind the method that won him so much success in business. He switched from von Clausewitz to Jomini, from strategic intuition to theory of change. Yet theory of change is not bad in itself. Weiss played a heroic role in overcoming the great resistance of social agencies to measuring results. Yet hypothesis testing is only half the story, and it's the second half. Weiss does not tell us how to come up with a hypothesis in the first place. She just wants you to make sure to test your hypothesis. But success in social enterprise depends on whether your hypothesis can be useful in practice, and that, in turn, depends on the examples from history that combine to make the hypothesis in the first place.

The what-works matrix accomplishes this first step of the scientific method that theory of change skips. The matrix came out of GE's training center at Crotonville, New York, in the 1990s. The GE CEO, Jack Welch, wanted a way to find and combine what works across the whole company: "The operative assumption is that someone, somewhere, has a better idea; and the operative compulsion is to find out who has that better idea, learn it, and put it into action—fast."[26] The company's chief learning officer,

Steve Kerr, used the matrix to do what Welch was after. Groups of GE managers came through Crotonville for training programs of various kinds. Kerr gave each group a real-time GE situation to tackle while they were there. They used the what-works matrix to do it.[27] Let's see how the matrix works and then how it applies in a recent example of social enterprise.

Here is Kerr's matrix.

Situation? (draft)					
Sources? (draft)	I	2	3	4	Etc.
Solution? (draft)					
Element A					
Element B					
Element C					
Element D					
Etc.					

You start on the first line, where you state your understanding of the situation or problem, hypothesis, or goal. The matrix says "draft" because your understanding will likely change as you proceed. Next, list what you think the elements of a solution are, that is, what you have to do well to solve the problem. These are in draft too. Then you ask the most important question you can ever ask, to solve any problem of any kind: Has anyone ever made any progress solving any pieces of this puzzle? You then list these sources across: 1, 2, and so on. These too are in draft.

Now the treasure hunt begins. You look in the sources for elements that work and fill in the matrix as you find them. You don't try to fill in the whole matrix. You stop when a combination strikes you as promising enough to try. At that point you've found your hypothesis. It is fine too if you do the exercise and find nothing worthwhile: you can't force discovery. In an honest search it's possible to come up empty-handed. It happens to scientists all the time. At some point you might decide to stop searching and move on to a different problem.

The what-works matrix is of recent vintage. After Welch and Kerr left GE in early 2001 the practice died out at GE. In social enterprise we have only one example so far of applying the matrix in a formal way. Still, in this instance we can see how the matrix fits better the scientific method than Weiss's theory of change.

Our example comes from the aftercare program of a family foundation in Florida.[28] *Aftercare* is a term in the social sector for programs that help people reenter normal life after some form of setback, such as drug addiction or major surgery. Here, we will deal with aftercare for children coming out of jail. In most cases juvenile jails are more like strict camps than adult prisons. The goal of this kind of aftercare is to prevent kids from getting into trouble again and going back to the juvenile jail.

The Florida family foundation funded programs in aftercare for children and wondered how to do it better. Instead of sponsoring an evaluation of what they funded, in 2003 the foundation asked the same question as GE: What works? To find out they commissioned a scan of aftercare for children in Florida and elsewhere. The result was a what-works matrix, shown on the next page.

"JJ" means juvenile justice. Note the $25-per-day limit. The treasure hunt found that was the realistic ceiling for what state governments would pay nonprofits for these services. Note too the absence of sources across the table. That's because the hunt found so little treasure. There are precious few sources worth stealing from. Instead, the whole list of elements that existing agencies put in place showed a woeful shortage of good results. In aftercare there was no good hypothesis to test.

The hunt led instead in a different direction. On the following page is the what-works matrix for that.

The treasure hunt turned from aftercare to the whole juvenile justice system. It found plenty that worked, so much that not everything fit on the matrix. To save space, the sources appear scattered inside the boxes rather than across the top. The measure

JJ Aftercare on $25/Day: What Works?

PROGRAM	IMPACT ON RECIDIVISM
Caseworker/probation officer advocacy and advice	Not effective
Curfews	Not effective
Reporting to day centers	Not effective
Check-ins with probation officer, sometimes intensive	Not effective
Military drills	Not effective
Random drug tests	Not effective, but big constituency
Electronic monitoring	Not effective
Probation rule enforcement	Not effective, seen as way to get youth back into system
Tutoring	Shaky data
Help to enroll in alternative schools	No evaluation, experts say depends on quality of school
Help to find a job	No data, experts say depends on job
24/7 crisis intervention phone number or beeper	No data
Anger management classes	Not effective, depends on accurate assessment of youth needs
Groupwork: reality therapy, positive peer culture	Not effective
Keep busy after school & weekends (e.g., sports)	Slightly effective, if linked to good mentoring like boys/girls clubs
Traditional social work	Not effective
Community service or internships	Evidence weak
Help to find a mentor (e.g. big brother or sister)	Boys/girls clubs have modest effect
Job readiness skills classes	Sometimes
Life-skills classes	Yes, but not alone
Help to find independent living arrangements	Maybe

JJ System Improvement: What Works?				
Keep more kids out of the system	Annie Casey's A1 pilots	Wraparound Milwaukee	Quantum opportunities	Civil citation
Deal with family problems	Functional family therapy (FFT)	Multi-Systemic Therapy (MST)	Brief Strategic Family Therapy (BSFT)	County placement during residential (e.g. Missouri)
Deal with behavior/mental problems	Aggression replacement therapy	High-dose intensive cognitive therapies	Some life skills curricula help a bit	Multi-modal therapeutic interventions
Deal with education problems	Reading 180	Maya Angelou boarding school	Dade County School	Comprehensive K-12 school reform
Service provider quality improvement	Florida's in-house proposals	Washington Stage, 1997: Community Juvenile Accountability Act		
Long-term transition to adulthood	The way	Teaching family homes	Treatment foster care	
Job training	Home builders, youth builders	Bay Point School, Miami	Gulf Coast Trade Center	
Independent living	Maya Angelou boarding school	Bay Point School, Miami		
Managing the multi-stream funding mess	Connecticut JJ Coalition for Reform	Missouri	Wraparound Milwaukee	
Sustainable financing of community care	Ohio: RECLAIM	Wraparound Milwaukee		
Overall orientation of bureaucratic system	Missouri	Connecticut Juvenile Justice Alliance	Idaho: FFT as part of reentry	Washington Stage, 1997: Community Juvenile Accountability Act

of success stayed the same from the previous aftercare matrix, namely, cost-effectiveness and a low rate of children going back to juvenile jail. But instead of stand-alone aftercare programs, what happens after release shows up on the new matrix as part of a larger system. For example, instead of going to prison, kids in Missouri go to campus schools near enough home to encourage family visits, and the same counselors stay in touch when the child gets out and goes back to the family.

The Florida foundation circulated a report that gives the details of what they found. It funded a series of meetings to spread what works to the myriad social agencies and funders in the Florida juvenile justice system. In that way everyone is literally on the same page. On that page there is plenty for every agency in Florida to find a combination of elements that works for them. And there is plenty to take up together too. For instance, the matrix includes a multiagency Milwaukee collaboration that was so successful that the managers of the juvenile jails complained they could no longer fill their beds.

Progress in Florida will take some time, but the early signs are good. The Florida legislature is already considering reforms that would put the state-run part of the system in the same league as the states that appear in the matrix: Missouri, Washington, and Connecticut. Whatever the eventual outcome in Florida, the aftercare example shows a working alternative to *Strategic Planning Workbook* and Weiss's theory of change for social programs. We see how strategic intuition can fit into formal methods of research, planning, and evaluation, thanks to GE's what-works matrix.

Yet it is not just their formal appeal that makes the methods of *Strategic Planning Workbook* and Weiss so popular. There is another reason too, perhaps the most important. Their methods conform to the common, romantic view of how great things happen in social enterprise:

Dream big. Work hard.

Strategic Planning Workbook does not dispute that. It just adds a step:

Dream big. Work hard. Adjust.

Same with Weiss. She adds a step too:

Dream big. Work hard. Measure results.

And what does strategic intuition say?

See how. Dream big. Work hard.

Repeat.

9

Picasso Dines with an African Sculpture

Creative Combination in the Professions

Strategic intuition is good business. It's scientific. But is it creative?

Combining past examples might seem just mechanical. Intelligent memory as a warehouse with elements coming off the shelves to fit together—it sounds like Sears filling a catalog order. Where's the creativity in that?

The word *create* has two meanings: to bring something into existence and to produce through imaginative skill.[1] Schumpeter's notion of creative destruction fits the first definition: entrepreneurs create. The key creation that strategic intuition produces is the strategy itself. That's what the strategist brings into existence. It is a creative act by the first definition. The second definition applies to creative artists. So far, none of our strategists has been very artistic.

Does this mean that strategic intuition and artistic creativity are two different things? The most common view of how artists work is through imagination, originality, and self-expression—not by combining past elements. Art comes from inside you, not from combining elements from others. This common view applies not just to pure art but to the many professions that call for some kind of artistic skill. Most big companies have creative departments for product design and marketing. Some firms specialize in these creative tasks. These firms depend on artistic creativity to some degree. Are all these forms of artistic creativity exempt from strategic intuition?

To answer this question let's study how artists work. We take as an example Pablo Picasso, the most famous artist of the twentieth century. At first glance his art looks utterly original, nothing at all like anyone else's. Picasso's art seems to have come from inside him. Picasso arrived at his signature style sometime between two self-portraits of 1901 and 1907. The earlier one, *Self-Portrait with Cloak*, shows a bearded figure in black clothes against a blue background. If you stand back, it looks realistic, like a photograph. That's not the Picasso who changed the world of art. The later one, called simply *Self-Portrait*, features the distorted shapes and unrealistic colors of the famous Picasso style. At once you know it as a Picasso. From 1901 to 1907, how did Picasso create his new style?

There is no doubt that Picasso was born with great artistic talent. From an early age, growing up in Spain, he showed skill in drawing far beyond his years. But he was certainly not born with his distinctive style, as the 1901 self-portrait shows. He created that new style in Paris, where he moved to in 1900 at the age of nineteen. He lived a bohemian life in the Bateau Lavoir, which was a building filled with artist studios. A *bateau lavoir* was a boat on the Seine River where laundresses took the laundry to wash and hang, and the studio building gained that name from all the laundry the artists hung out to dry, as they were too poor to pay a laundress. Picasso's roommate was Max Jacob, a fellow painter who later became a writer. Through 1906 Picasso tried various styles, all in the previous traditions of realism and impressionism.

Then Picasso discovered Henri Matisse. In the summer of 1905 Matisse had the first great breakthrough of modern art. His new paintings created a stir at a fall exhibition in Paris. Over the next winter Matisse painted his first masterpiece of the new style, *Happiness of Life*. It created an even greater stir at a spring exhibition in 1906. For the first time Matisse won a contract to supply one of the leading art dealers of Paris, Eugène Druet. It was a major step forward for the new style of art. The key features of Matisse's new style were distorted shapes, unrealistic colors, and a flat look without shading or lines of perspective.

Meanwhile, Picasso had some minor success, enough to win the Steins as admirers: Gertrude, her brothers Leo and Michael, and Michael's wife Sarah. Now Picasso went to see *Happiness of Life*, and the Steins brought Matisse to visit Picasso's studio. The two painters met again in the Stein apartment. That was the night that Picasso found his style.

Matisse brought along his daughter, Marguerite, who worked as his assistant. He also brought along an African sculpture. This was the heyday of colonialism, when African art became one of the exports back to Europe. Paris artists started to collect sculpture especially and admired it for technical reasons, especially how the sculptures conveyed great beauty through angular, distorted shapes. Matisse's biographer, Hilary Spurling, reports what happened next:

> Picasso reacted fast. He dined with the Matisses, refusing to be parted all evening from the statue, and staying up afterwards in his studio in the Bateau Lavoir, where Max Jacob found him next morning surrounded by drawings of a one-eyed, four-eared, square-mouth monster which he claimed was the image of his mistress.[2]

Picasso had a flash of insight. The timing reveals the elements he combined: Matisse's *Happiness of Life* and the African sculpture. The result was his breakthrough masterpiece, *Les Demoiselles d'Avignon*. In Picasso's painting you see the same key elements from Matisse's new style: distorted shapes, unrealistic colors, and a flat look without shading or lines of perspective. Even the colors are similar—beige and reddish brown—and so are the postures of the women. Yet the two paintings also look very different: the African sculpture adds a rough, angular look to Picasso's, in clear contrast to Matisse's gentle curves.

This kind of creative combination is an open secret in the art world. Artists have a word for the act of stealing: *influence*. This nicely shifts the spotlight: Matisse influenced Picasso. That sounds better than "Picasso stole from Matisse." Yet artists know what really goes on. Harold Bloom struggled with the psychology of stealing in his classic work, The Anxiety of Influence. Even Shakespeare, one of the great thieves of all time, worried in his early days about stealing so much from Marlowe.[3]

Once you start noticing that artists steal, the examples are endless. E. L. Doctorow's 1975 novel Ragtime took its plot and even the name of its main character—Kohlhaus became Coalhouse—from a German novel of 1810 by Heinrich von Kleist.[4] In March 2007 The New York Times reported a new music CD by Josef Mysliveček:

> "Mozart was indeed a master imitator, capable of working in a large variety of styles," Maynard Solomon writes in his biography Mozart: A Life. It was a skill Mozart was proud of. In Mysliveček, Mozart found a model of the Italianate style and its graceful melodies and elegant rhythms. He borrowed ideas from Mysliveček's works for his first opera seria, "Mitridate," and themes for early symphonies of his own. He arranged a Mysliveček aria, which became the popular "Ridente la calma," and was for a time considered the composer of Mysliveček's oratorio "Abramo ed Isacco."[5]

Strategic intuition works the same way in art as it does in other fields. Innovation comes through creative combination, by bringing past elements together in a new and useful way. That does not diminish Picasso's talent. It simply explains a key feature of what that talent entails. The combination is unique because Picasso is unique. The elements that make up the combination are not unique at all.

Yet the belief that art is different—that creativity comes from within—led to the invention of a host of techniques for stimulating imagination across the modern professions. There are three general categories of creative methods at work: for individuals, for groups, and for your work environment. First, each person needs to be creative. Second, each team needs to be creative together.

Third, your whole company needs a creative atmosphere that stimulates rather than stifles the creative energy of individuals and teams. Let's look at these three kinds of methods to see if they foster strategic intuition.

Let's start with the first category, creativity for individuals. Here are three methods for that:

> The Wishing Technique . . . requires participants to look squarely at a problem . . . and ask, "If I could have this happen any way I want, how would it be?" Then, they describe exactly what would occur. . . . The purpose . . . is to create an unlimited approach to thinking, which may lead to a breakthrough.
>
> Image Streaming . . . is . . . if you state the problem clearly, close your eyes, and begin describing all the images and actions you see, you can interpret them like dreams. It's a way of letting your subconscious do the work.
>
> The Sensory Involvement Technique . . . [has] people analyze their sales presentation and ask, "Is there some other sense we can appeal to—sound, color—that we may be missing?"[6]

These three techniques reveal the common misunderstanding that creative ideas come from wishes, the subconscious, or the five senses. None of these three methods directs you to examples from history as the source of creativity. And they do not encourage presence of mind. They are forms of concentration, not clearing your mind. In applying your presence of mind you clear away even the problem because the solution that strikes you might solve a different problem.

These three techniques are typical of most individual methods for stimulating creativity. Wishing, the subconscious, and the five senses are ways to think out of the box. But the best way to think out of the box is to look in other boxes. You search widely for elements that work, with an open mind about what problem you might actually be able to solve. It's discovery, not imagination, that makes you more creative.

Beyond these individual techniques group methods for creativity often include team-building exercises too. For example, a group builds a race car out of duct tape and toilet paper rolls. This may help create bonds in the group, but it is not the same as creative thinking. It is unlikely that this will help anyone come up with a new idea once the workshop is over. The tape or rolls never figure as elements in the real-life problems the team may face. Such activities are fun, and they might help build teams and might make you more receptive in the future to other people's ideas, but they do not yield creative ideas you can actually use.

By far the most popular group technique for stimulating creative ideas is brainstorming. There are two common forms. In a simpler form of brainstorming you drop in at someone else's office to toss around ideas. That's a very good thing to do. For strategic intuition other people are great sources for examples from history to combine. The second, more complex form of brainstorming is a formal meeting where members of a team throw out ideas to solve a problem. This is not a good thing to do.

The word *brainstorming* entered the English language in 1953, thanks to *Applied Imagination*, a popular book by Alex Osborn. As the head of an advertising firm in the 1930s, Osborn worried that when he met with his managers they brought up boring ideas. So he took to inviting younger staff to join the meetings. This worked. The younger people did great. Brainstorming seemed to unleash their creativity.[7]

There is no doubt that Osborn's new format got better results. But why? Osborn thinks the format itself stimulated everyone's imagination. But perhaps something else was going on: the junior staff already had good ideas and the meeting gave them a chance to pass those ideas on to Osborn without his managers blocking them. Brainstorming sessions are an excellent way to bypass bureaucracy without offending the managers in the middle. That's good. But that does not mean the format of brain-storming stimulates creative ideas.

Ask around your office. Ask your friends. When do they have their best ideas? They will seldom answer, "During a brainstorming session." More likely it was at night or in the shower or while stepping onto a train or while stuck in traffic or while daydreaming in a meeting about something else entirely. So we are not surprised when Dr. George Lopez tells us how he founded his company, ICU Medical, that makes a new kind of IV device. It was in the hospital, on an ordinary day. An IV tube slipped out, and the patient died. Dr. Lopez went to call the patient's wife. He noticed the phone jack in the wall:

> "This is crazy," Lopez thought. "If this comes out, all I lose is a call, yet it's more secure than the IV." That night he sketched out a new system with a locking device to keep the tube in place. . . . ICU Medical has captured nearly 10 percent of the global IV market.[8]

You can't schedule creative combination. Intelligent memory works twenty-four hours a day, every day, even in sleep. Who knows when a combination will strike you? Despite this basic human experience you find that your manager has scheduled a session from 3:00 P.M. to 5:00 P.M. next Wednesday for the team to come up with creative ideas. But that's not how innovation works.

Brainstorming has grown with the spread of formal methods of strategic analysis and strategic planning—from Jomini to Porter—because these methods offer no other way of coming up with a strategy. You study your situation—and then what? In the absence of further guidance the planning team gets together to brainstorm ideas on what action to take. It's the most important part of strategy, and here you rely on brainstorming: a two-hour meeting with everyone tossing ideas off the top of their heads.

Even the army resorts to brainstorming for arriving at a strategy. *Field Manual* 5-0 is their standard guide to planning and problem solving for officers of every rank. You do your situation analysis and then you generate options:

> Brainstorming is the preferred technique for generating options. It requires time, imagination, and creativity, but it produces the widest range of options. The staff remains unbiased and open-minded in evaluating proposed options.[9]

Osborn would approve. Certainly it is good to look at all options with an open mind. Yet 5-0 gives us no guidance on how to come up with an option in the first place, other than imagination and creativity, which is nothing more than thinking out of the box again. In contrast, strategic intuition offers a way to come up with an option for action by looking into other boxes. And the aim should not be to come up with the widest range of options, to compare them all on an equal footing. Of course you should not accept every idea that strikes you. But you're looking for one idea, not many. When it strikes you other ideas take second place. You compare these others not all together, but one by one with your favorite. You might reject the others, favor another one over your own, combine elements from both, or end up rejecting all of the above and start again. That's how intelligent memory works.

Brainstorming rules the day in most professions. Instead of fighting against brainstorming we can try out versions that come closer to strategic intuition. For example, try reverse brainstorming. Schedule a weekly meeting where people can bring ideas that struck them over the previous week, on any topic at all. Traditional brainstorming forces you to solve a particular problem at a particular time, as in, "We will brainstorm about subject X at 3 P.M. next Wednesday." In contrast, reverse brainstorming lets people bring ideas on any subject that strike them at any time.

In traditional brainstorming the group picks out the best idea right then and there. In reverse brainstorming you don't decide right away. If you can bring an idea on any topic at all, the rest of the group might not have thought about that topic before. They greet your idea with a blank collective stare. So instead of evaluating your idea the group just asks you to explain the idea as best as you can, including the elements you combined to come up with the idea. Then everyone goes off to mull it over. The discussion continues informally in person, by telephone or via e-mail. Eventually, a promising idea might emerge from the pack. At that point, it's time for the what-works matrix, as an individual or group exercise. Or nothing emerges. That's fine. A week goes by, and the next reverse brainstorming meeting comes round.

In practice many teams do a version of reverse brainstorming, even though they call it brainstorming. The renowned design firm IDEO makes a conscious effort to bring existing elements from different fields to all its brainstorming meetings.[10] Consulting firms in all sectors typically include senior partners in brainstorming sessions, precisely to draw on elements from their past assignments. So converting from ordinary to reverse brainstorming might not be very hard. The key is to take advantage of your brain making connections all through the week, not just in a two-hour meeting.

Beyond individual and group methods of creativity these days there are many popular methods for building a creative work environment. One of the most famous of these environments is Google's new Manhattan office. An online city blog, Gothamist, gives us a guided tour:

> Gothamist went on an official tour, complete with watching a game of ping-pong, getting a sneak peak at the famous lunch, and waving at scooter riders whizzing down the hallways, making it by far one of the coolest places to work in Manhattan. . . . [The . . .] floor plan evolved to include approximately four micro kitchens equipped with snacks, a game room, idea boards, a lecture hall, two cafés, majestic ten-foot-tall windows, and conference rooms named for New York City landmarks. . . . Facilities Manager Laura Gimple . . . says, "I think it's so fun because there is no limit, anything is possible because we are such a creative environment . . . the employees can really express themselves." That creativity is evident throughout the building.[11]

It sounds like fun. But still we ask: What does this all have to do with creativity? There is no research to support the idea that this kind of environment makes people more creative in their work. The playful environment certainly makes them feel more creative, but feeling creative and producing creative results are not the same thing.[12] You're more productive when you like your work environment, but productive does not equal creative. It is hard to see how games and cafés and scooters let employees express themselves and create a physical space where there is no limit and anything is possible.

Let's remember how the Google guys came up with their creative ideas. The origin of Google had nothing to do with having fun or expressing themselves. Page and Brin did not believe that there were no limits and that anything was possible. Page and Brin got their creative ideas from combining existing elements. How does the new Google office help their employees do that?

Two features seem to help. First, the Google office environment invites lots of breaks. That's good for presence of mind. When you're stuck on a problem, a game of Ping-Pong is an excellent way to free your mind. Second, idea boards everywhere help you capture ideas as they come to you and let others see them too. Still, there is nothing that encourages Google staff in the specific technique of combining existing elements.

The Google office resembles nothing so much as a college dorm but with better architecture, better equipment, and better food. Most Google employees are young, so they feel at ease in that environment. But let's not confuse that with creativity. A practitioner of Zen could make the opposite argument: the most creative work environment is a blank, empty box. You don't want Ping-Pong or a watercress salad to distract you from freeing your mind completely. In the end we have no way to measure whether being busy or being blank is better.

All the leading methods for creative ideas—from wishing, imaging, and sensing for individuals, to brainstorming for groups, to a playful work environment—spring from the same fallacy: the two-sided brain. You take off your analytical hat and put on your creative one. The two-sided brain dates back to Roger Sperry's 1981 Nobel Prize and had two decades of widespread popularity until Eric Kandel won the Nobel Prize in 2000. It will take some time for the whole-brain model of intelligent memory to have a similar influence in offices around the world.

We recall that even at the time of his Nobel Prize, Sperry acknowledged that the split-brain model might not hold up in future research. As science started to move beyond the dual brain, but before the triumph of intelligent memory, other models of creative intelligence appeared. One of the models suggests that there are not two hats—analytical and creative—but many. In *Six Thinking Hats* (1985) Edward de Bono picks the white hat for analytical thinking, red for emotional thinking, black for pessimistic thinking, yellow for optimistic thinking, green for creative thinking, and blue for procedural thinking.[13] As with the dual brain, intelligent memory overturns this idea of multiple modes of thought. But as of today de Bono's hats remain popular.

In a similar vein Howard Gardner proposed multiple intelligences in 1983.[14] At first count, Gardner came up with seven intelligences: linguistic, logical–mathematical, musical, spatial, bodily kinesthetic, interpersonal, and intrapersonal. Later he added an eighth intelligence, naturalistic, and as of 2005 considered a ninth, existential.[15] Like de Bono's hats, Gardner's intelligences remain popular, although intelligent memory overturns both models of multiple modes of thinking. The whole brain works as one, not as Sperry's two or de Bono's six or Gardner's eight.

On the other hand, Gardner did a great service in helping to weaken IQ as a measure of innate intelligence. He claims that IQ measures at most two kinds of intelligences: linguistic and logical–mathematical. If you do poorly on an IQ test, you might still be very intelligent, but in one of the six or seven other intelligences that the test does not measure. But it is intelligent memory that deals the deathblow to IQ: from the moment you're born, your memory starts building. Because no two people have

identical experience, no two people have identical brains. We cannot sort out what is innate and what is the result of memory from
the time you were born. IQ measures your current ability to take
a certain kind of test. But it does not measure innate intelligence.
No one knows how to do that.[16]

Likewise, no one can measure creative intelligence. We simply can't distinguish creative thinking from other kinds of intelligence, whatever color hat we wear. Only the basic workings of
intelligent memory account for our single mode of thought. You
take in elements on the shelves of your brain, and they come
together in new combinations. To make more new combinations
and to be more creative, you need to put more things on the
shelves of your brain and free your mind to let them connect.

We end this chapter with a famous example of a creative
method that seems to defy intelligent memory: *Drawing on the
Right Side of the Brain* (1979) by Dr. Betty Edwards. This book has
become a standard in the field of art teaching. In a revised edition, ten years after, Edwards reported:

> Over the past decade, the ideas I expressed about learning to
> draw have become surprisingly widespread, much to my amaze-
> ment and delight. College and high school art teachers, even junior
> high and elementary school teachers across the nation have incor-
> porated many of the techniques into their teaching repertoires.
>
> Even more surprising, individuals and groups working in fields
> not remotely connected with drawing have found ways to use
> the ideas in my book. A few examples will indicate the diversity:
> nursing schools, drama workshops, corporate training seminars,
> sports-coaching schools, real-estate marketing associations, psy-
> chologists, counselors of delinquent youths, writers, hair stylists,
> even a school for training private investigators.[17]

Edwards claims that her method helps you to be creative in any
profession. If the claim is true, we wonder how can that happen
with just the right side of the brain. There is no doubt that her

method works. But if this method is a split-brain technique, then the method seems to contradict strategic intuition. Let's take a closer look to find out.

In the first chapter of her book, Edwards presents before-and-after drawings by students she taught. These drawings are truly astounding: the early pictures are childish and crude and the later ones elaborate and fine. In most cases this change took only three months. Edwards explains:

> Most of the exercises in the book are intended to increase your ability to draw *realistically*—that is, to enable you to see and draw some object or person in the real world with a high degree of similarity to the observed image.[18]

Edwards teaches you to draw like a camera. That is hardly the kind of creative self-expression we expect from Sperry's version of the right side of the brain. But Edwards is after something else: to turn off your words and draw what you see. Sperry taught her that words come from the left side of the brain and images come from the right side of the brain. So she wants you to turn off the left side and turn on the right side.

Edwards does succeed in helping you to turn off your words and draw what you see. From intelligent memory we know that seeing versus thinking has nothing to do with the right or left side of the brain. So a modern title for Edwards's book might be, *Draw What You See, Not What You Think*. If we ignore the part about the left and right brain, Edwards does give us a creative method, for art and other professions.

Here's how it works. Take any photograph. Put your drawing paper beside it. Draw lines to divide the photograph into quarters. Do the same for your drawing paper. Now turn the photograph upside down. In the upper left quadrant of your paper, draw what you see in the upper left quadrant of the photograph. Then do the same for the other three quadrants. Turn your drawing right side up. You'll be amazed at how well you drew.

Edwards's method works because your brain is normally so good at fitting elements together—the basic mechanism of intelligent memory. If the photograph shows a Roman arch, and you see a curve that looks like it's made of bricks, your brain says the word *arch* because you have an arch on the shelves of your mind. Then you go ahead and draw the picture of the arch on your shelf, not the arch you actually see. That's bad. Even worse, every time you draw an arch it comes out the same way. So that image of an arch on the shelves of your brain gets stronger and stronger each time.

To correct the mistake, you make the arch disappear. That's what happens when you turn the photograph upside down. Now your brain can no longer recognize the arch. All you see is a bunch of shapes. You give no name to the shapes. Your brain does not say "arch." Now you draw what you actually see, not the arch on the shelves of your brain. When you're done, you turn the drawing right side up. Now you see the arch. But it's not the one on the shelves of your brain. It looks like the one in the photograph.

Edwards goes on to give various versions of this basic technique for real scenes rather than photographs and for students of different ages and levels of skill. By the end of her training you can turn off your words and concepts without any effort. It becomes a normal way for you to look at the world around you. This is very hard to achieve, so it's no surprise that you need her lessons to do it.

To justify her method, Edwards does not need the split-brain model. Intelligent memory explains it quite well. And like Sperry himself, Edwards recognized that the split-brain model might not hold up:

> In short, the method works, regardless of the extent to which future science may eventually determine exact location and confirm the degree of separation of brain functions in the two hemispheres.[19]

Toward the end of her book we find a different theory that holds up better. In Chapter 12, "The Zen of Drawing," Edwards's method promotes presence of mind as we know it in strategic intuition, or beginner's mind in the Zen tradition. She trains you to look at something—a photograph, a face, or a landscape—and free your mind of all words and concepts about the object. Drawing only what you see suspends all thought. It is the same kind of meditation we find in Asian martial arts and philosophy. Edwards shows us a way to achieve the same state quickly, anywhere, with only a pencil and paper.

And so we can add Edwards's drawing technique to our list of creative methods across professions. We now have three creative methods at our disposal. Reverse brainstorming captures ideas no matter when they strike. The what-works matrix helps you search for elements to make up a solution, as an individual or a team. And Edwards gives a shortcut to beginner's mind. All three methods foster strategic intuition. As we saw from Picasso, that's how creativity works, even in modern art.

10

Do We Do Dewey?

Teaching Strategic Intuition

John Dewey is the most famous educator of the twentieth century. Starting with *My Pedagogic Creed* in 1897, to his death in 1952, Dewey led the shift from traditional to progressive methods of instruction. Instead of lecturing students on theories and facts the teacher guides them in self-directed discovery.

Today you find progressive methods from nursery school through graduate school. Harvard Business School applies these methods to teaching business in general and strategy in particular. Their famous case method "redefines the traditional educational dynamic in which the professor dispenses knowledge and students passively receive it."[1] They put Dewey's essay, "Thinking in Education," at the front of their handbook, *Teaching and the Case Method*.[2] A champion of the case method at Harvard Business School, C. Roland Christensen, explains that a case teacher's job is not to direct students to "the answer" but rather to engage in "questioning, listening, and response." Christensen contrasts this method with traditional education:

> Yet much of our education system reinforces "getting the answer" as the ultimate goal of learning.... While no instructor can revolutionize the academy single-handedly, each of us can improve his or her own practice.[3]

Is this the best way to teach strategic intuition? Such a nontraditional subject seems to call for nontraditional methods. We might assume that teaching students to think, rather than to absorb facts and theories that give the right answer, would build their strategic intuition. After all, strategy is about an unknown future, where we don't know the right answer until after the future unfolds. Even then we cannot measure whether another strategy would have done better because all strategic situations are different and we can't repeat the experiment. It might seem that strategy is precisely where progressive thinking skills would work better than traditional facts and theories.

So says the earliest guide to the Harvard case method, *The Case Method of Instruction* (1931). The lead essay by Arthur Dewing, a Harvard professor of finance, explains it as follows:

> Education ... deals with the oncoming new in human experience rather than with the departing old.... The ... accumulation of human experience does not necessarily involve thinking, because the accumulation of human experience is inevitably the taking of what is given rather than the creation of what is new. If we teach people to deal with the new in experience, we teach them to think.... In any event, all a teacher can hope to do is to develop, first, an appreciation of the almost infinite complexity of modern business problems, second, the hopelessness of reaching a definite and unequivocal solution, and third ... the solution of this dilemma by some carefully reasoned but, in the end, common-sense line of action.[4]

Dewing wrote at a time when progressive education was just taking off. Thomas Kuhn was in fourth grade at a progressive school when Dewing's essay came out. Kuhn remembers:

> I started my education—or started going to school, which is another matter—in New York, in Manhattan. And I was there for some years in progressive school, from kindergarten and then on through the fifth grade. Progressive school encouraged a sort of independent thinking. On the other hand, it didn't do much to

teach subject matter. I remember at a time I was probably already in second grade, my parents were getting discouraged because I didn't seem to be able to read; my father held letters up for me and then I got on to it pretty fast.[5]

Kuhn did not consider his schooling to be real "education" because his school did not teach him subject matter. For Kuhn, the scientific method starts with a profound respect for past achievements—tradition—that the scientist then combines in a flash of insight. That was what Kuhn did himself when he had his breakthrough on Aristotle.

For science education Kuhn goes further. Textbooks that summarize past scientific achievements are "immensely effective" and leave the scientist "almost perfectly equipped" for "puzzle solving within the tradition that the textbooks define". Then, to "switch from paradigm to paradigm"—as a flash of insight does—you must read the original works of the scientists who made those achievements, such as "Newton, Faraday, Einstein, or Schrödinger."[6]

Kuhn, one of our key sources on strategic intuition, comes down clearly against progressive education and in favor of an ultratraditional education with textbooks and original works. A flash of insight draws on elements from the past. You must study the past to put these elements on the shelves of your brain.

This respect for the past seems counter to the Harvard case method. The next page shows a list of model questions that Christensen asks in a case discussion. None of these questions directs the student to past achievements. There are no past theories, tools, ideas, or examples, and there is nothing about what the key individuals thought and did in the case itself. Instead, Christensen asks what the student thinks and what the student would do in the future. This is a far cry from Kuhn telling you to read Isaac Newton in the original.

Yet the origins of the case method tell a different story. The case method started at Harvard Law School in the early nineteenth century, when legal education took the form of apprenticeship.

Open–ended questions	"What are your reactions to the General Motors case?" "What aspects of this problem were of greatest interest to you?" "Where should we begin?"
Diagnostic questions	"What is your analysis of the problem?" "What conclusions did you draw from these data?"
Information-seeking questions	"What was the gross national product of France last year?"
Challenge (testing) questions	"Why do you believe that?" "What evidence supports your conclusion?" "What arguments might be developed to counter that point of view?"
Action questions	"What needs to be done to implement the government's antidrug campaign?"
Questions on priority and sequence	"Given the state's limited resources, what is the first step to be taken? The second? And the third?"
Prediction questions	"If your conclusions are correct, what might be the reaction of the Japanese auto industry?"
Hypothetical questions	"What would have happened to the company if a strike had not been called by a union?"
Questions of extension	"What are the implications of your conclusions about the causes of the Boston bottling plant strike for executives in plants in other large cities?"
Questions of generalization	"Based on your study of the computer and tele-communications industries, what do you consider to be the major forces that enhance technological innovation?"[7]

You worked in a law firm and learned the practice from more senior lawyers. As the law grew more complex formal education spread through the professions. Legal training moved out of the law offices and into the classroom. There it lost the connection with real practice. So in the 1870s Dean Christopher Columbus Langdell brought practice to Harvard law students in the form of real documents from past cases. This study of previous examples especially fit American common law in the English tradition, where judges base their rulings on past cases and evolving social norms rather than on the strict body of prescriptive law that continental Europe inherited from the Napoleonic Code.[8]

The study of what opposing lawyers and judges wrote in actual cases where we see who won and lost, and why, comes close to Kuhn's study of exactly what Newton or Einstein did and said about their achievements. But it's a far cry from Christensen's list of questions. In the century between Langdell and Christensen the case method shifted its gaze from what the case subjects thought and did to what the students think to do.

The cause of the shift was progressive education. Dewey came after Langdell and before Christensen. It was Dewey who put the student, not the past, at the center of instruction. The modern version of the Harvard case method looks directly to Dewey for its theory of how to teach strategic thinking. To understand the implications of progressive education for strategic intuition, let's take a close look at what exactly Dewey proposed.

Dewey earned his Ph.D. in philosophy at Johns Hopkins, where Professor G. Stanley Hall lectured on the principles and methods of intellectual training, starting with children, especially the training of attention of will. Another Hopkins professor, Charles Peirce, was a founder of American pragmatism. Dewey began his career in education applying Peirce's pragmatic philosophy to Hall's problem of the right way to teach philosophy to children.[9]

For Dewey *philosophy* is not an academic discipline but a means for an individual to make sense of the world and convert that sense into action of all kinds. It's very much like *strategy*. Pragmatism fits the four steps of von Clausewitz, where you pick and choose from theories as needed to solve a particular problem. American pragmatism first applied to religion, in the face of many creeds mixing and clashing in the new country. Which one to choose? All of them, in whatever combination suits your personal situation.[10] We hear a modern echo of this spirit in a recent description of Alan Greenspan, longtime head of the Federal Reserve, who took elements from various economic theories and combined them as needed in "pragmatic eclecticism."[11]

Dewey applied pragmatism to education in much the same spirit. In 1916 he produced his great work, *Democracy and Education: An Introduction to the Philosophy of Education*:

> The theory of the method of knowing which is advanced in these pages may be termed pragmatic ... so as to enable us to adapt the environment to our needs and to adapt our aims and desires to the situation in which we live.[12]

Von Clausewitz would approve, especially in adapting aims and desires to the situation rather than putting those first as Jomini does. So far Dewey fits right in with strategic intuition.

In 1894 Dewey moved to the University of Chicago. There he began a University Elementary School as a laboratory for his methods. His biographer Jay Martin reports:

> Planting, growing, harvesting, and cooking what is produced, weaving to create useful household items, sewing to create and repair garments, woodworking to create socially useful products, writing for communication instead of penmanship, drawing or painting to convey emotions, counting numbers to maintain accounts, reading the stars to learn directions, resting for restoration—these were activities designed to develop the children's talents in relation to their social use. . . . A child in Dewey's school was instantly a member of a cooperative commonwealth.[13]

Although Dewey called all this *pragmatic*, others called it *progressive*, in keeping with the Progressive Era of social reform in America at that time. There is a strong element of utopian commune in Dewey's new school. But the curriculum itself is pragmatic, in the sense that students learn to do something useful first and then gain formal knowledge to understand it and do it better. Each student is different in some way, so each student's pragmatic path to learning is different too. The key to progressive education is individualized instruction, where the teacher helps each student find the best path.

Dewey's new method was a world away from common practice at the time. Elementary education was a version of adult education: the teacher lectures to students in rows on material far removed from their everyday experience. For young children this was absurd. Dewey overturned that model. He moved to Columbia University in 1904, and from there his influence spread throughout the country. New York City especially became a hotbed of progressive education, in part because it was a hotbed of progressive social movements in general. Columbia's Teachers College and, from 1916, the Bank Street School taught generations of teachers the new progressive methods.

Two decades after *Democracy and Education* Dewey wrote a follow-up, *Experience and Education* (1938). In it he explains:

> Mankind likes to think in terms of extreme opposites. It is given to formulating its beliefs in terms of Either-Ors, between which it recognizes no intermediate possibilities.... At present, the opposition ... tends to take the form of contrast between traditional and progressive education.[14]

Dewey goes on to judge that the progressive education movement got it only half right:

> [F]inding the material for learning within experience is only the first step. The next step is the progressive development of what is already experienced into a fuller and richer and also more organized form, a form that gradually approximates that in which subject-matter is presented to the skilled, mature person.[15]

Dewey never endorsed lecturing to children in rows, but he did want to teach them traditional subject matter, progressively. You introduce each subject gradually, a little at first to very young children and then more as they progress. That's what he meant by progressive education:

> [T]he sound idea that education should derive its materials from present experience and should enable the learner to cope with the

problems of the present and the future has often been converted into the idea that progressive schools can to a very large extent ignore the past.... But the achievements of the past provide the only means at command for understanding the present....

[T]he ongoing movement of progressive education fails to recognize that the problem of selection and organization of subject-matter for study and learning is fundamental. Improvisation that takes advantage of special occasions prevents teaching and learning from being stereotyped and dead. But the basic material of study cannot be picked up in a cursory manner. Occasions which are not and cannot be foreseen are bound to arise whenever there is intellectual freedom. They should be utilized. But there is a decided difference between using them in the development of a continuing line of activity and trusting to them to provide the chief material of learning.[16]

For Dewey traditional subject matter, in the form of past achievements, provides the chief material of learning. But you must combine that material from the past with progressive methods in a student's early years. When Dewey started his career, education consisted of traditional content and traditional methods. He wrote his first big book in 1916 about progressive methods. Then the progressive movement adopted these methods, including the Harvard case method, but threw out the traditional content. Dewey corrected this error in 1938, to restore the balance of traditional content and progressive methods. But by then it was too late. Progressive education was already an industry and very hard to change.

Kuhn would approve of Dewey's respect for past achievements in the content of education. In his memoirs, Napoleon agreed:

[t]actics can be learned through treatises, somewhat like geometry, and so can the various evolutions of the science of the engineer and the gunner; but knowledge of the grand principles of warfare

can be acquired only through the study of military history and of the battles of the great captains and through experience.[17]

Napoleon sounds a lot like Kuhn. Napoleon tells us that in order to be successful you combine the knowledge conveyed by textbooks (treatises) with past achievements, including your own.

Von Clausewitz offers further advice on how to use the grand principles—the theory—of whatever field you study:

> Theory is instituted that each person in succession may not have to go through the same labor of clearing the ground and toiling through his subject, but may find the thing in order, and light admitted on it. It should educate the mind of the future leader in War, or rather guide him in his self-instruction, but not accompany him to the field of battle; just as a sensible tutor forms and enlightens the opening mind of a youth without, therefore, keeping him in leading strings all his life.[18]

Learning past theories and examples prevents you from reinventing the wheel or from making the same mistakes as others who came before you. But those past theories and examples can't tell you what action to take in any particular situation. The past theories and examples do not accompany you onto the battlefield. For von Clausewitz, only coup d'oeil gives you the precise combination of strategic elements in any particular situation.

Napoleon, von Clausewitz, Kuhn, Langdell, and Dewey all endorse studying the past. Progressive education and the case method do not. Christensen's advice on what a teacher should do reads a lot like Dewey's warning about what a teacher should not do.[19]

Still the case method does draw from the past in one way. It gives students real-life examples from history of companies and leaders in action. The students put these examples on the shelves of their brains as future elements to draw on. But this is not an explicit aim of the case method or its teachers. Most written cases in the case method are not the original documents and original thinking of the subjects themselves, as in Langdell's case materials. Case method cases today are typically essays where the author weaves together what happened and then asks the student to recommend a future course of action. This gives the students a lot of information about the industry and company, but they get too little detail about what the case subjects thought and did.

Robin Hogarth offers a solution to this modern case problem. In a review of recent research, *Educating Intuition* (2001), Hogarth proposes an explicit method for producing and teaching examples from history. He finds the method in the field of medicine, where a tradition of grand rounds placed patients in the hands of expert doctors in front of an audience of other doctors. The expert doctors talked out loud their sequence of thoughts, and the audience listened to the questions the experts asked of the patients. Charles Abernathy and Robert Hamm adapt this as a written method of professional scripts in *Surgical Intuition*.[20] Hogarth contrasts these scripts with the case method:

> It should be emphasized that professional scripts are quite different from the case studies that are so popular in business schools. . . . As is typically used in business schools, the case study is not a way to build good intuitions for solving business problems. There is no clear criterion that distinguishes good from bad decisions. The experience is superficial, and it offers little chance to learn from expert practitioners.[21]

Hogarth's professional scripts add another piece of the puzzle for teaching strategic intuition. You teach students how strategic intuition works, plus you give them the traditional subject matter of your discipline, and you give them plenty of professional scripts. This provides past examples to draw from and the understanding of how they combine to form useful ideas.

There is still one key step in strategic intuition that these methods of education do not treat directly: presence of mind. Here we harken back to Asian martial arts, where techniques from the Hindu, Buddhist, and Zen traditions help you achieve beginner's mind for every strategic situation. Recently magnetic resonance imaging (MRIs) of Buddhist monks show how these monks achieved beginner's mind. Sharon Begley reports on this research in her 2007 book *Train Your Mind, Change Your Brain*, as a "ground-breaking collaboration between neuroscience and Buddhism."[22] Neuroscientists increasingly recognize the scientific merit of Buddhist methods: Begley's book features a foreword by the Dalai Lama, leader of Tibetan Buddhism and winner of the 1989 Nobel Peace Prize. The Dalai Lama also gave the inaugural lecture at the annual meeting of the Society for Neuroscience in November 2005.

Meditation is the basic technique for creating presence of mind. Yoga adds body positions and martial arts add rigorous movements. Classes in these methods have become very popular among adults. You find them now even in schools, to help children develop mental discipline. The same discipline for presence of mind proves useful in two everyday situations: when you reach a dead end on a problem or when you feel negative emotions. Both situations result from strategic error, where you misjudged the Karma against you and chose a Dharma that did not work. With enough practice you can learn to change your mental state at any time, without sitting down to meditate or doing the movements of yoga or martial arts.[23]

All in all it is possible, in theory, to teach the elements of strategic intuition. In practice, over the past three years Columbia Business School has pioneered just such a course. We can't calculate results directly by testing students before and after on their skill because we have no way to measure strategic intuition. But student satisfaction is high, and the course has quickly become one of the most popular in the school. Here's a sample comment:

Upon reflection of our class discussions and the assigned readings I can't help but feel a profound difference in the way I think and feel about strategy. Prior to this class it didn't occur to me that there was any alternative to the traditional Jominian approach (even though I never previously heard of Jomini!). The concept of setting a goal and then creating a plan to achieve that goal has been so beaten into us since we were children. Our parents and teachers have always told us to aim high, set goals, and work hard to achieve those goals. And what a failure if we decided to change goals! Von Clausewitz and the notion of strategic intuition is a breath of fresh air that should be taught to every high school and college student as a life tool and business students as an approach to business strategy. (C. Gottesman, pers. comm.)[24]

Young people without much experience can develop both expertise and strategic intuition. Napoleon won his first battles when he was twenty-six years old—about the same age as most graduate students. He had no experience but plenty of expertise from his formal military education and strategic intuition from his study of great generals who came before him. You don't just rely on your own experience. You draw from the rest of the world as well. Strategic intuition might increase with age and experience—at least its potential does—but the right education can make it grow faster.

11

Kennedy Shoots for the Moon

Progress Through Opportunity

America gave the world the philosophy of pragmatism and also its opposite.

Our pilot course on strategic intuition begins with students picking which statement they agree with more, A or B.

A	B
You can achieve anything you want if you believe in yourself, set clear goals, and work hard.	You can achieve many things if you prepare for opportunity, see it, and act on it.

Pragmatism and strategic intuition lead to B. But most students answer A. In workshops with business executives, army officers, and nonprofit leaders the results are the same: A. Non-Americans tend to answer B more, but the longer they've been in America the more they seem to answer A.

Why is this? Once you read through A word by word you cannot possibly agree with it. Where did this idea come from? It clearly has a strong appeal. There must be something to it despite its apparent error.

The precise origin is very hard to pin down. In written form we can go back to Horatio Alger's stories of poor boys rising in life through hard work, courage, virtue, and determination. Alger wrote dozens of these tales, from 1867 until his death in 1899. He was the most popular American author of his time. In most of his tales a boy rises from nothing to a good job in a good company, usually with the help of a rich older man, as reward for some self-less deed. But we also find Alger's 1881 biography of James A. Garfield, *From Canal Boy to President*,[1] a true story of a poor boy who became the president of the United States. Overall Alger's boys became folk heroes of the rags-to-riches, can-do American dream.

The tradition continues well into the twentieth century, with advice attached to the stories, in the form of books such as Napoleon Hill's *Laws of Success* (1928), Norman Vincent Peale's *The Power of Positive Thinking* (1955), and Anthony Robbins's *Unlimited Power* (1987).[2] Robbins and his many imitators run popular workshops to drive the message home: with the right attitude and a lot of hard work, you can achieve anything you want. The good side of this tradition helps you develop a positive feeling about yourself and what you can achieve. The problem arises when you move from a feeling to actual strategy: your dreams must conform to reality, to the particular Karma you face.

Horatio Alger and his descendants endorse the can-do American spirit, but they did not invent it. The earliest source seems to be the legend of Columbus, our first great American dreamer. When the United States won its independence a popular movement arose to rename the country "Columbia" in his honor versus the colonial name "America." In the end only the capital, District of Columbia, took the new name. Columbus does stand out in the history of human achievement but for reasons very different from the legend itself.

Columbus dreamed of sailing west from Europe to Japan. Portuguese and Spanish scholars argued that he could not possibly do it. The scholars knew from astronomy the distance around the Earth, and they knew from Marco Polo's journals the distance from Spain to Japan. The scholars calculated that sailing west from Spain would take forty-five weeks to reach Japan. In those days a ship could carry supplies for only nine weeks of sailing. The scholars concluded, correctly, that Columbus would run out of supplies long before he completed the journey of forty-five weeks. Columbus did not listen. He presented his own calculations that showed Japan was only nine weeks away. Those calculations were wrong. But the Spanish king and queen sided with Columbus. After nine weeks at sea Columbus struck land. To his dying day he believed it was Japan. Despite his colossal error and blind luck, Columbus became the first hero of the great American dream.

Columbus serves as an amazing example of A, not B, in our opening exercise. But what does that tell us about human achievement? We find much to admire in his positive attitude and determination. But do we really want to ignore all evidence from past experience and set out across the ocean, hoping for an unknown continent to suddenly appear and save us?

The Columbus legend took off for another reason too. America became a prosperous place where poor Europeans found no feudal system to hold them down. The tremendous economic growth of America in the nineteenth and twentieth centuries made these Europeans rich far beyond the prospects they left behind. Recent immigrants from other continents find the same thing. In America, for vast numbers of people, dreams really have come true.

A more recent version of the Columbus legend is President Kennedy's race to the moon. He had an impossible dream. His determination made it come true. In his book *The Moon and the Ghetto* (1977) the economist Richard Nelson asked why America can't achieve as much in the social realm.[3] Thirty years later Nelson continues to work on the problem at the Consortium for Science, Policy & Outcomes. Nelson recalls:

Many years ago, I got interested in what people were then calling "the moon and the ghetto" problem. This was the commentary in the late 1960s: "If you can land a man on the moon, why can't you solve the social problems of the ghetto?"[4]

To answer this question we need to look back to the origin of Kennedy's strategy. Did the idea for landing a man on the moon

come from an ambitious dream, or was it yet another case of strategic intuition?

On May 25, 1961, after four months in office, Kennedy gave a
speech on Urgent National Needs to both houses of Congress. He
announced to them and to the world:

> I believe that this nation should commit itself to achieving the goal,
> before the decade is out, of landing a man on the moon and return-
> ing him safely to the earth. . . . But . . . it will not be one man going
> to the moon—it will be an entire nation. For all of us must work to
> put him there.[5]

And so began the Apollo program. It succeeded on July 20, 1969,
when Neil Armstrong set foot on the moon. That was six months
ahead of Kennedy's deadline. It was a thrilling example of a dream,
a clear goal to make it come true, a great effort to reach the goal,
and a success right on schedule. Surely this is A, not B.

But from our study of strategic intuition we still want to know
how Kennedy got the idea. In the same speech to Congress he
also said:

> Recognizing the head start obtained by the Soviets with their large
> rocket engines, which gives them many months of lead-time, and
> recognizing the likelihood that they will exploit this lead for some
> time to come in still more impressive successes, we nevertheless
> are required to make new efforts. For while we cannot guarantee
> that we shall one day be first, we can guarantee that any failure to
> make this effort will find us last.[6]

At the time of Kennedy's speech the Soviet Union already had
the goal of landing on the moon. As Kennedy said, the Soviets
had many months of lead time. The Soviets sent the first object
into orbit—*Sputnik* on October 4, 1957—and the first human
into space and into orbit—Yuri Gagarin on April 12, 1961. Two
days after Gagarin's flight the U.S. House Committee on Science

and Astronautics called an urgent hearing. Here is an exchange between Congressman David King of Utah and Robert Seamans of NASA:

KING: I understand the Russians have indicated at various times that their goal is to get a man on the Moon and return safely by 1967, the fiftieth anniversary of the Bolshevik Revolution. Now specifically I would like to know, yes or no, are we making that a specific target date to try to equal or surpass their achievement?

SEAMANS: ... our dates are for a circumlunar flight in 1967 and a target date for the manned lunar landing in 1969 and 1970.

KING: ... then that outlines the issue very squarely. As things are now programmed we have lost.[7]

Before Kennedy became president, NASA already had a plan to land on the moon, and the Saturn rocket was the means to get there. The German rocket scientist Werner von Braun developed the Saturn, starting in 1957. The plan to reach the moon advanced in the Eisenhower years. In January 1961, two weeks before Kennedy's inauguration, George Low led a NASA team to lay out the steps in detail: one astronaut for a short earth orbit in 1961, three astronauts for longer orbits in 1965, three astronauts for a moon orbit in 1967, and a moon landing in 1968–1971. This was the timing that in the hearings King of Utah declared too late.[8]

A few days after the hearings Kennedy wrote a memo to his vice president, Lyndon Johnson, asking:

1. Do we have a chance to beat the Soviets by putting a laboratory in space, or by a trip around the moon, or by a rocket to land on the moon, or by a rocket to go to the moon and back with a man. Is there any other space program which promises dramatic results in which we could win?

2. How much additional would it cost?

3. Are we working 24 hours a day on existing programs. If not,
   why not? If not, will you make recommendations to me as to
   how work can be speeded up.[9]

In the end Kennedy decided to go for the moon landing. He was
clearly on a pragmatic search for the best combination of existing
elements, especially the Saturn rocket. A month and a day after his
memo Kennedy made his big speech. He and NASA expected the
Soviets to get to the moon in 1967 and the United States two years
later. Neither the goal to land on the moon nor the plan to get there
was Kennedy's idea. His speech was a request to Congress for extra
funds to speed up the plan. Nobody knew at the time that the Soviet
Union would miss their target and never reach the moon.

Kennedy did not dream the impossible. He brought forward
elements from the past that showed the way to a reachable goal.
He looked for a dramatic program where he had the means to
succeed. It was a fine example of pragmatism in action. That's B,
not A, in our opening exercise. Yet Kennedy's move took personal
courage, in line with Albert Einstein's advice to a young scientist:
"One must develop an instinct for what one can just barely achieve
through one's greatest efforts."[10] Kennedy displayed that instinct,
which we recognize now as strategic intuition. And Kennedy had
the resolution to overcome the obstacles that stood in the way of
achieving his goal.

The Columbus legend, the Alger stories, the immigrant dream,
Kennedy's race for the moon, and the writings of Hill, Peale, and
Robbins all give you a positive message about striving for success.
They inspire you to persevere and keep your chin up in the face
of adversity. That's good. But for strategy the popular understanding of these stories gives you the wrong idea. These stories imply
that you can do anything and that when you do succeed it's all
because of you. It's an appealing philosophy because it ignores
all outside forces. When things go well you have only yourself
to thank. But if you don't achieve your dreams, you have only
yourself to blame. When things go badly you go back to another

Alger book or another Robbins workshop for another dose of the can-do spirit.

To rescue the can-do idea for strategy we convert our idea of America from a place where dreams come true to a land of opportunity. Of course these opportunities are limited and specific. If we could give the A–B exercise to Americans during the Great Depression, they would likely have answered "neither." It was not a time when you could achieve "anything you want" (A) or even "many things" (B). In those days you could achieve very few things. A few Americans, of course, achieved great success even then, but by finding specific opportunities and not by following their dreams.

Nelson's question—If we can reach the moon, why can't we solve social problems?—takes us back to the same answer as in our other examples of human achievement. You look to specific opportunities, not ambitious dreams, to find the way ahead. Progress follows where achievements take it, not where you want it to go. Evolution in nature works in a similar way, with no set direction beyond the sum of the adaptations of all the species on earth. But human achievement adds an extra element. Innovation in nature comes from a random gene mutation in new offspring, while in humans the innovation comes from a flash of insight in a specific human mind.

Progress in human affairs comes through opportunity, when someone sees it, seizes it, and turns it into reality. We cannot predict what opportunities will arise and whether anyone will see them, so we cannot predict the course of human progress. But at least we know how that progress works. We have seen how strategic intuition appears in and applies to a wide range of fields, through centuries and around the world. Flashes of insight tell a hidden story of human achievement. In all the cases we studied the opportunity for achievement arose not just as an opening, like a gap in the wall. It came as a combination of past elements that can fill the opening as well. Without those elements the opportunity does not exist.

My opportunity to write this book arose when I saw a gap in the field of strategy at the same time that I saw the existing elements that might combine to fill that gap. In all these chapters not a single idea, not a single example, is my own. I borrowed them all. But the combination is new, and I am grateful for the opportunity to present it here to you.

Notes

Preface

1. See William Duggan, *Napoleon's Glance: The Secret of Strategy* (New York: Nation Books, 2002); William Duggan, *The Art of What Works: How Success Really Happens* (New York: McGraw-Hill, 2003).

1. Flash versus Blink

1. Malcolm Gladwell, *Blink: The Power of Thinking Without Thinking* (New York: Little, Brown & Co., 2005).

2. Eknath Easwaran, *Bhagavad Gita* (New York: Vintage, 2000); Sun Tzu, *The Art of War* (Oxford: Oxford University Press, 1994); Miyamoto Musashi, *A Book of Five Rings* (New York: Overlook, 1992).

3. Carl von Clausewitz, *On War* (New York: Penguin, 1968).

4. Thomas Kuhn, *The Structure of Scientific Revolutions* (Chicago: University of Chicago Press, 1962).

2. Revolution on Earth

1. Thomas Kuhn, *The Structure of Scientific Revolutions* (Chicago: University of Chicago Press, 1962).

2. Thomas Kuhn, *The Copernican Revolution* (Cambridge: Harvard University Press, 1957), 140–142.

3. Ibid., 181.

4. Kuhn, *Structure*, 11.

5. Roger Bacon, *Opus Majus*, ed. J. H. Brodges (Oxford: Clarendon Press, 1897–1900), cited in Joseph Campbell, *The Hero with a Thousand Faces* (Princeton: Princeton University Press, 1968), via Lynn Thorndike, *History of Magic and Experimental Science* (New York: Columbia University Press, 1958).

6. Peter Galison, *Einstein's Clocks, Poincare's Maps: Empires of Time* (New York: Norton, 2004), 199–200, 218. Christopher Jon Bjerknes details everything Einstein borrowed from others but mistakenly criticizes Einstein for it, in *Albert Einstein: The Incorrigible Plagiarist* (Downers Grove, IL: XTX, 2002). Einstein described his own flash of insight in a lecture in Japan in 1922, later translated into English from Japanese notes by Yoshimasa A. Ono, in "How I Created the Theory of Relativity," *Physics Today*, v. 35, n. 8, August 1982.

7. Kuhn, *Structure*, 122–123.

8. Thomas Kuhn, *The Road Since Structure* (Chicago: University of Chicago Press, 2000), 16–17. This quote comes from a paper Kuhn presented in 1981.

9. Werner Heisenberg, cited in David Cassidy, *Uncertainty: The Life and Science of Werner Heisenberg* (New York: Freeman, 1992), 228.

10. William James, *Pragmatism: A New Name for Some Old Ways of Thinking* (New York: Longman Green, 1907), 58.

11. Ibid., 54.

3. Two Halves of a Brain

1. Roger W. Sperry, "Nobel Lecture" (lecture, Stockholm Concert Hall, Stockholm, December 8, 1981).

2. We find W.J.'s story in Joseph E. Bogen and Philip Vogel, "Cerebral Commissurotomy in Man," *Bulletin of the Los Angeles Neurological Society* 27, no. 4 (December 1962), and in a series of articles by Bogen, Sperry, and Sperry's research assistant, Michael Gazzaniga: Michael S. Gazzaniga, Joseph E. Bogen, and Roger W. Sperry, "Some Functional Effects of Sectioning the Cerebral Commisures in Man," *Proceedings of the National Academy of Sciences of the United States of America* 48 (1962): 1765–1769; Michael S. Gazzaniga, Joseph E. Bogen,

and Roger W. Sperry, "Laterality Effects in Somesthesis Following Cerebral Commissurotomy in Man," *Neuropsychologia* 1 (1963): 209–215; Michael S. Gazzaniga, Joseph E. Bogen, and Roger W. Sperry, "Observations on Visual Perception After Disconnexion of the Cerebral Hemispheres in Man," *Brain* 88, no. 2 (June 1965): 221–236.

3. Joseph E. Bogen, "The Neurosurgeon's Interest in the Corpus Callosum," in *A History of Neurosurgery*, ed. Samuel H. Greenblatt (Park Ridge: American Association of Neurological Surgeons, 1997). The ghostly color, the central location, and its role in connecting the parts of the brain to make a whole led early brain scientists to posit the corpus callosum as the seat of the human soul.

4. Roger W. Sperry, "Cerebral Organization and Behavior," *Science* 133, no. 3466 (1961): 1749–1757.

5. Michael S. Gazzaniga, "Forty-Five Years of Split-Brain Research and Still Going Strong," *Neuroscience* 6 (August 2005): 653. It seems that Gazzaniga had tried to study Van Wagenen and Herren's original patients in Rochester with a new set of experiments, after Andrew J. Akelaitis there reported no great effect from cutting the corpus callosum. Gazzaniga got a second chance when he became Sperry's assistant at Caltech.

6. Jerre Levy-Agresti and Roger W. Sperry, "Differential Perceptual Capacities in Major and Minor Hemispheres," *Proceedings of the National Academy of Sciences of the United States of America* 61, no. 3 (1968): 1151.

7. Sperry, "Nobel Lecture"; ibid.

8. Seiji Ogawa et al., "Brain Magnetic Resonance Imaging with Contrast Depending on Blood Oxygenation," *Proceedings of the National Academy of Sciences of the United States of America* 87 (December 1990): 9868–9872; Seiji Ogawa et al., "Functional Brain Mapping by Blood Oxygenation Level-Dependent Contrast Magnetic Resonance Imaging. A Comparison of Signal Characteristics with a Biophysical Model," *Biophysical Journal* 64 (March 1993): 806 (Figure 1).

9. As with Aristarchus in astronomy, there was a scientist who came up with a key idea to solve the problem of how thought actually happens. In *The Mneme* (1904), Richard Semon argued that nerve cells firing in a certain pattern leave a memory in the brain. Daniel Schacter invokes Kuhn to explain why science of the time ignored Semon so thoroughly that he had no influence on later scientists who validated similar ideas with experimental data. It did not help that Semon thought you inherit memories from your parents. See Richard Semon, *The Mneme* (New York: Macmillan, 1921); D. Schacter, *Forgotten Ideas, Neglected Pioneers: Richard Semon and the Story of Memory* (Philadelphia: Psychology Press, 2001).

10. Brenda Milner, "Les Troubles de la Memoire Accompagnant les Lésions Hippocampiques Bilatérales," in *Physiologie de l'Hippocampe* (Paris: Centre

national de la recherche scientifique, 1962), translated into English in Peter M. Milner and Steven Glickman, *Cognitive Processes and the Brain* (Princeton: Van Nostrand, 1965).

11. Eric Kandel, "Nobel Lecture" (lecture, Stockholm Concert Hall, Stockholm, December 10, 2000). In 1967, Kandel started studying the giant sea slug. It grows to about two pounds and a foot high on the bottom of the ocean off the coast of California. Its brain has 20,000 cells, compared to 1,000,000,000,000 cells in a human brain. But those brain cells are the largest in the animal kingdom—big enough to see with the naked eye. That allowed Kandel to study the chemistry and physiology of an individual brain cell over time as the slug went about its life.

12. Barry Gordon and Lisa Berger, *Intelligent Memory: Improve the Memory that Makes You Smarter* (New York: Viking, 2003), 8–9. See also Gerald Edelman, *Wider Than the Sky: The Phenomenal Gift of Consciousness* (New Haven: Yale University Press, 2004).

13. See Brenda Milner, L. Squire, and E. Kandel, "Cognitive Neuroscience and the Study of Memory," *Neuron* 20 (1998): 445–468; Larry R. Squire and Eric R. Kandel, *Memory: From Mind to Molecules* (New York: Scientific American, 1999). For an example of recent research, see Mark Jung-Beeman et al., "Neural Activity when People Solve Verbal Problems with Insight," *PLOS Biology* 2, no. 4 (2004): e97.

14. For research on this mechanism and how past elements combine in the brain to form a new strategy, see Demis Hassabis et al., "Patients with Hippocampal Amnesia Cannot Imagine New Experiences," *Proceedings of the National Academy of Sciences of the United States of America* 104, no. 5 (January 2007): 1726–1731; Alan Hampton and John O'Doherty, "Decoding the Neural Substrates of Reward-related Decision Making with Functional MRI," *Proceedings of the National Academy of Sciences of the United States of America* 104, no. 4 (January 2007): 1377–1382. In the first study, at University College London, it was found that injury to the hippocampus harms not just recall of the past but also projections into the future. Patients could not imagine new experiences even in familiar scenes such as a pub or a beach. In the second study, at Sperry's own CIT, MRIs of a simple decision-making task identified the combined signals from three different brain regions to solve the problem.

4. Lieutenant M Saves Your Life

1. Gary Klein, *Intuition at Work: Why Developing Your Gut Instincts Will Make You Better at What You Do* (New York: Currency, 2003), xv.

2. Gary Klein, *Sources of Power: How People Make Decisions* (Cambridge: MIT Press, 1998), 2–3.

3. Klein, *Intuition at Work*, xv.

4. Ibid., xvi.

5. Ibid., xv.

6. See Part 4, "Chess," in *Human Problem Solving*, ed. Allen Newell and Herbert A. Simon (Englewood Cliffs, NJ: Prentice Hall, 1972).

7. Herbert A. Simon, *Models of Thought: Volume 2* (New Haven, CT: Yale University Press, 1989), 187.

8. Ibid., Chapters 4.2–4.6.

9. Ullrich Wagner, Steffan Gais, Hilde Haider, Rolf Verleger, and Jan Born, "Sleep Inspires Insight," *Nature* 427 (2004): 352–355.

10. Klein, *Sources of Power*, 125.

11. Ap Dijksterhuis, Maarten W. Bos, Loran F. Nordgren, and Rick B. van Baaren, "On Making the Right Choice: The Deliberation-Without-Attention Effect," *Science* 311 (February 2006): 1005–1007.

12. See, for example, Steven Sloman and David Lagnado, "The Problem of Induction," in *Cambridge Handbook of Thinking & Reasoning*, ed. Keith J. Holyoak and Robert G. Morrison (New York: Cambridge University Press, 2005), 95–116.

13. Steven Sloman, "The Empirical Case for Two Systems of Reasoning," *Psychological Bulletin* 119, no. 1 (1996): 7. Used with the kind permission of the author. Steven Sloman cites a dissent from Paul Smolensky, "On the Proper Treatment of Connectionism," *Behavioral and Brain Sciences*, 11, no. 1 (1988): 1–23. Smolensky has gone on to work on a single mode of thought or "a unified theory of cognition" that "integrates connectionist and symbolic computation," as he says on his Web site at Johns Hopkins University, http://www.cog. jhu.edu/faculty/smolensky/#Papers. See also Paul Smolensky and Géraldine Legendre, *The Harmonic Mind: From Neural Computation to Optimality-Theoretic Grammar* (Cambridge: MIT Press, 2006).

14. Brenda Milner, Larry R. Squire, and Eric R. Kandel, "Cognitive Neuroscience and the Study of Memory," *Neuron* 20, no. 3 (March 1998): 445–468. For a summary of cognitive research and theories on flashes of insight that precede the advances in neuroscience of intelligent memory, see Robert J. Sternberg and Janet E. Davidson, *The Nature of Insight* (Cambridge: MIT Press, 1995).

5. The Corsican Conquers Europe

1. Carl von Clausewitz, *On War* (New York: Penguin, 1968/1832), 366. The most common translation in English is Colonel James John Graham's, from

1873. Both von Clausewitz's original German text and Graham's translation use the French term in the main discussion of coup d'oeil in Book 3. In Book 8, Graham uses coup d'oeil, but the German original appears as "Überblick," which literally means *overglance* and figuratively means overview or mental grasp. It is likely that von Clausewitz used Überblick as the closest German translation of coup d'oeil. See Carl von Clausewitz, *Vom Kriege* (Bonn: Dümmlers, 1980), 950. The term *coup d'oeil* was well known in military circles thanks to Frederick the Great of Prussia, who used it in a narrow sense of an eye for the lay of the land. See Frederick II, King of Prussia, "Article 6: Of the Coup d'Oeil," in *Military Instruction from the Late King of Prussia to His Generals* (London: Egerton, 1797).

2. J. Christopher Herold, *Mind of Napoleon: A Selection of His Written and Spoken Words* (New York: Columbia University Press, 1955), 224.

3. For a fuller treatment of these four steps, see William Duggan, *The Art of What Works: How Success Really Happens* (New York: McGraw-Hill, 2003), 22–26.

4. Antoine Jomini, *Summary of the Art of War* (Washington, DC: Military Service Publishing, 1947).

5. Edward Earle, *Makers of Modern Strategy: Military Thought from Machiavelli to Hitler* (Princeton, NJ: Princeton University Press, 1943), 89, cited in John R. Elting, "Jomini: Disciple of Napoleon?," *Military Affairs* 28, no. 1 (Spring 1964): 23.

6. For a fuller treatment of these three steps, see Duggan, *Art of What Works*, 16–18.

7. Herold, *Mind of Napoleon*, 221.

8. Carlo D'Este, *Patton: A Genius for War* (New York: HarperCollins, 1995), 94.

9. William Sulis and Allan Combs, *Nonlinear Dynamics in Human Behavior* (Amsterdam: IOS Press, 2000); Christopher Beekman and William Baden, *Nonlinear Models for Archaeology and Anthropology: Continuing the Revolution* (London: Ashgate, 2005); Manuel De Landa, *A Thousand Years of Nonlinear History* (Cambridge: Zone, 1997).

10. Alan Beyerchen, "Clausewitz, Nonlinearity, and the Unpredictability of War," *International Security* 17, no. 3 (Winter 1992): 59–90.

11. William Duggan, "Coup d'Oeil: Strategic Intuition in Army Planning," U.S. Army War College, Strategic Studies Institute, November 2005.

6. Warrior Buddha

1. There are many excellent modern translations if you want to consult the classic texts. I used Samuel Griffith's translation of *The Art of War* (Oxford: Oxford

University Press, 1984); Stephen Mitchell's translation of *Tao te Ching* (New York: HarperCollins, 1988); Eknath Easwaran's translation of *Bhagavad Gita* (New York: Vintage, 2000); and Victor Harris's translation of *Book of Five Rings* (New York: Overlook, 1992). See also R. King, *Indian Philosophy* (Edinburgh: Edinburgh University Press, 1999); William Theodore De Bary, *The Buddhist Tradition: India, China and Japan* (New York: Vintage, 1972); and Daisetz T. Suzuki and William Barrett, *Zen Buddhism* (New York: Doubleday, 1996).

2. In Indian texts the flash of insight is *pratibha* (Sanskrit) and in Zen texts it is *satori* (Japanese). Here is a modern version of the story: "Gotama . . . progressed through ever higher states of consciousness until he gained an insight that forever transformed him. . . . But there seems little new about this insight, traditionally known as the Four Noble Truths and regarded as the fundamental teachings of Buddhism. . . There seems nothing strikingly original about these truths. Most of the monks and ascetics in North India would have agreed with the first three. . . . He had not made this up; it was not a new creation of his own. On the contrary, he always insisted that he had simply discovered 'a path of great antiquity, an ancient trail, traveled by humans in a far-off, distant era.' " Karen Armstrong, *Buddha* (New York: Viking, 2001), 81–82. Note that the flash is slow—it took a long time to come together in Buddha's mind—and none of the elements are new. But that exact combination is new, at least in words. Buddha was not the first to achieve enlightenment: he was the first to describe the method simply and clearly to others.

3. Carl von Clausewitz, *On War* (New York: Penguin, 1968/1832), 142.

4. J. Christopher Herold, *Mind of Napoleon: A Selection of His Written and Spoken Words* (New York: Columbia University Press, 1955), 43, 240.

5. Sun Tzu, *The Art of War*, 109, 93, and 101.

6. See Daisetz Teitaro Suzuki, *Zen Mind, Beginner's Mind* (New York: Weatherhill, 1970).

7. Gates and the Google Guys Go for It

1. Michael Porter, *Competitive Strategy: Techniques for Analyzing Industries and Competitors* (New York: Free Press, 1980); Michael Porter, *Competitive Advantage: Creating and Sustaining Superior Performance* (New York: Free Press, 1985).

2. Thomas Davenport and Laurence Prusak, *What's the Big Idea? Creating and Capitalizing on the Best New Management Thinking* (Boston: Harvard Business School Press, 2003), 77.

3. Bill Gates, *The Road Ahead* (New York: Viking, 1995).

4. Ibid., 16.

5. Robert X. Cringely, *Accidental Empires: How the Boys of Silicon Valley Make Their Millions, Battle Foreign Competition, and Still Can't Get a Date* (Boston: Addison Wesley, 1992), 102.

6. Gates, *The Road Ahead*, 17.

7. Ibid., 20.

8. Ibid., 12.

9. Ibid., 229.

10. Ibid., 15.

11. For VisiCalc, see http://www.bricklin.com/history/saiidea.htm. For e-mail, see http://openmap.bbn.com/~tomlinso/ray/firstemailframe.html. It was the same for the earlier era: FORTRAN came from "English shorthand and algebra" in 1957, according to Steve Lohr, "John W. Backus, 82, Fortran Developer, Dies," *New York Times*, March 20, 2007.

12. David Vise, *The Google Story: Inside the Hottest Business, Media, and Technology Success of Our Time* (Westminster, MD: Dell, 2005).

13. Ibid., 36.

14. Ibid., 37.

15. Ibid., 38.

16. Ibid., 41. AltaVista itself came from previous elements: Flaherty combined a Web crawler and a scalable index.

17. Vise, *The Google Story*, 41–42.

18. Ibid., 69.

19. Ibid., 87–88.

20. Ibid., 88.

21. Triumph of the Nerds, directed by Bob Cringely. Performed by Douglas Adams, Sam Albert, and Paul Allen (Portland, OR: Oregon Public Broadcasting, 1996).

22. Triumph of the Nerds is the title of the three-film series, and *Great Artists Steal* is the title of the film with the Jobs interview.

23. T. S. Eliot, *The Sacred Wood* (London: Methuen, 1980), 125.

24. Gary Wolf, "Steve Jobs: The Next Insanely Great Thing," *Wired*, February 1986.

25. Lou Gerstner, *Who Says Elephants Can't Dance? Inside IBM's Historic Turnaround* (New York: Collins, 2002).

26. Ibid., 10.

27. Ibid., 16.

28. Ibid., 4.

29. On his first day Gerstner asked fifty top IBM managers, "Is there not some unique strength in our ability to offer comprehensive solutions, a continuum of

support? Can't we do that and also sell individual products?" Gerstner, *Who Says Elephants Can't Dance?*, 23.

30. Gerstner, *Who Says Elephants Can't Dance?*, 129.

31. Ibid., 129–130.

32. Porter, *Competitive Strategy*, xiv.

33. Ibid., xx.

34. Citation of the Sveriges Riksbank Prize in Economic Sciences in Memory of Alfred Nobel, 2002. The first sentence of Kahneman's Nobel lecture gives equal credit to Amos Tversky, who sadly died six years before.

35. Daniel Kahneman, "Nobel Prize Lecture" (lecture, Stockholm Concert Hall, Stockholm, December 8, 2002).

36. Daniel Kahneman, Paul Slovic, and Amos Tversky, eds., *Judgment Under Uncertainty: Heuristics and Biases* (Cambridge: Cambridge University Press, 1982).

37. Ibid., 20.

38. Kahneman, "Nobel Prize Lecture."

39. Kahneman, Slovic, and Tversky, *Judgment Under Uncertainty*, 24.

40. For a recent review of the literature and evidence on economic prediction, see Nassim Taleb, *The Black Swan: The Impact of the Highly Improbable* (New York: Random House, 2007).

41. Clyde P. Stickney and Roman L. Weil, *Financial Accounting: An Introduction to Concepts, Methods and Uses*, 11th ed. (Mason: South-Western College Publishing, 2005), 217.

42. David M. Levine et al., *Statistics for Managers Using Microsoft Excel*, 4th ed. (Upper Saddle River, NJ: Prentice Hall, 2004), 159.

43. Robert Pindyck and Daniel Rubinfeld, *Microeconomics*, 6th ed. (Upper Saddle River, NJ: Prentice Hall, 2004), 154. Unfortunately, many economists make the distinction between risk and uncertainty and then use them interchangeably.

44. Joseph Schumpeter, "The Creative Response in Economic History," *The Journal of Economic History* 7, no. 2 (1947): 149–159; Joseph Schumpeter, "Change and the Entrepreneur," in *Change and The Entrepreneur, Postulates and the Patterns for Entrepreneurial History*, Harvard University Research Center in Entrepreneurial History (Cambridge, MA: Harvard University Press, 1949); Joseph Schumpeter, "The Process of Creative Destruction," in *Capitalism, Socialism and Democracy*, ed. Joseph Schumpeter (New York: Harper & Brothers, 1942). For more on Schumpeter and strategic intuition, see William Duggan, *The Art of What Works: How Success Really Happens* (New York: McGraw-Hill, 2003), 45–47, 58–59, and 138–139.

45. Clayton Christensen, *The Innovator's Dilemma: The Revolutionary Book that Will Change the Way You Do Business* (New York: HarperBusiness, 1997);

Richard Foster and Sarah Kaplan, *Creative Destruction: Why Companies that are Built to Last Underperform the Market—And How to Successfully Transform Them* (New York: Doubleday, 2001); Michael Raynor, *The Strategy Paradox: Why Committing to Success Leads to Failure (and What to Do about It)* (New York: Currency, 2007).

46. Amar Bhidé, *The Origin and Evolution of New Businesses* (New York: Oxford University Press, 2000).

47. Robert Higgins, *Analysis for Financial Management*, 7th ed. (New York: McGraw-Hill, 2003), 104.

8. Mouse, Minister, and Moneylender

1. Thomas Kuhn, *The Structure of Scientific Revolutions* (Chicago: University of Chicago Press, 1962), 163.

2. See Michael Porter and Mark Kramer, "Philanthropy's New Agenda: Creating Value," *Harvard Business Review* (November–December 1999); Michael Porter and Mark Kramer, "The Competitive Advantage of Corporate Philanthropy," *Harvard Business Review* (December 2002); and Michael Porter and Mark Kramer, "Strategy and Society: The Link Between Competitive Advantage and Corporate Social Responsibility," *Harvard Business Review* (December 2006).

3. Bryan Barry, *Strategic Planning Workbook for Nonprofit Organizations* (Saint Paul, MN: Wilder Foundation, 1997), 5.

4. Ibid., 6–7.

5. Ibid., 7.

6. For more on Alice Paul's strategy, see William Duggan, *Napoleon's Glance: The Secret of Strategy* (New York: Nation Books, 2002), Chapter 7. For details on Paul's suffrage campaign, see Christine Lunardini, *From Equal Suffrage to Equal Rights* (New York: New York University Press, 1986), and Inez Irwin, *The Story of Alice Paul and the National Woman's Party* (New York: Harcourt Brace, 1921).

7. See "A Militant General—Alice Paul," in Doris Stevens, *Jailed for Freedom* (New York: Boni and Liveright, 1920).

8. For details of the prison episode, see Stevens, *Jailed for Freedom*.

9. This account draws from the leading authorities on the civil rights movement: Taylor Branch, *Parting the Waters* (New York: Simon and Schuster, 1988); David Garrow, *Bearing the Cross* (New York: Morrow, 1986); Howard Zinn, *SNCC: The New Abolitionists* (Boston: Beacon Press, 1964); Adam Fairclough, *To Redeem the Soul of America* (Athens: University of Georgia Press, 1987); and Clayborne Carson, *In Struggle* (Cambridge: Harvard University Press, 1981). For Ella Baker, see Joanne Grant, *Ella Baker* (New York: Wiley, 1998); Joanne Grant, *Fundi* (video, 1991); and Duggan, *Napoleon's Glance*, Chapter 6.

10. "The Nobel Peace Prize for 2006," press release of the Norwegian Nobel Committee, Oslo, October 13, 2006.

11. www.grameen-info.org/bank/hist.html.

12. Mohammed Yunus, *Banker to the Poor* (New York: PublicAffairs, 1999); David Bornstein, *The Price of a Dream* (New York: Simon & Schuster, 1996); and Alex Counts, *Give Us Credit* (New York: Times Books, 1996). See also Duggan, *Napoleon's Glance*, chapter 9.

13. Yunus, *Banker to the Poor*, 34.

14. Ibid., 48.

15. Carl von Clausewitz, *On War* (New York: Penguin, 1968/1832), 243.

16. Yunus, 50.

17. Bornstein, *The Price of a Dream*, 41.

18. Ibid., 40.

19. Ibid.

20. www.grameen-info.org/bank/hist.html.

21. www.gatesfoundation.org/AboutUs/OurValues/GuidingPrinciples.htm.

22. See Angela Morris, "A Survey of Theories of Change Within Philanthropy" (master's thesis, School of Public Administration, Grand Valley State University, 2004).

23. Global Leaders Tomorrow, "Philanthropy Measures Up," *World Economic Forum* (January 2003), 4.

24. Carol Weiss, *Evaluation Research* (Upper Saddle River, NJ: Prentice Hall, 1998), 331, 335, 338.

25. Ibid., 55, 65.

26. Robert Slater, *Jack Welch and the GE Way* (New York: McGraw-Hill, 1998), 97.

27. See "Learning Culture 2: Stealing Shamelessly," in Robert Slater, *The GE Way Fieldbook* (New York: McGraw-Hill, 1999). This explanation also came from George Anderson, personal communication, April 2001, and Steven Kerr, personal communication, November 2001. General Electric called it the Trotter Matrix, named for Lloyd Trotter, the company executive who developed an earlier version.

28. See Lynn Ellsworth, "Better Treatment and Aftercare for Delinquent Youth" (Eckerd Family Foundation, September 2003)

9. Picasso Dines with an African Sculpture

1. *Oxford English Dictionary* (http://www.oed.com) gives these two meanings as "to bring into existence" and "to design." *Merriam-Webster* (http://www.

m-w.com/dictionary) gives them as "to bring into existence" and "to produce through imaginative skill."

2. Hilary Spurling, *The Unknown Matisse: A Life of Henri Matisse*, vol. 1, 1869–1908 (London: Hamish Hamilton, 1998), 391.

3. Harold Bloom, *The Anxiety of Influence: A Theory of Poetry* (New York: Oxford University Press, 1997), 8.

4. John Disky, "The German Source of *Ragtime*: A Note," *Ontario Review* 4 (Spring–Summer 1976): 84–86.

5. Daniel Wakin, "A Composer Forgotten to All but Mozart," *The New York Times*, March 4, 2007.

6. These techniques come from Mattimore Communications, cited in B. Voss, "What's the Big Idea?" *Sales & Marketing Management* July (1991): 36–41.

7. Alex Osborn, *Applied Imagination* (New York: Charles Scribner's Sons, 1953). Osborn is the "O" in the great advertising firm BBDO.

8. Siri Schubert, "From Phone Line to Lifeline," *Business* 2.0, October 2, 2006, 50.

9. United States Department of the Army, *FM 5-0: Army Planning and Orders Production*, January 2005, 3.124. See also William Duggan, "Coup D'Oeil: Strategic Intuition in Army Planning," Strategic Studies Institute, U.S. Army War College, November 2005.

10. Andrew Hargadon, *How Breakthroughs Happen: The Surprising Truth About How Companies Innovate* (Boston: Harvard Business School Press, 2003).

11. "Gothamist Goes to Google," Gothamist.com, February 19, 2007, http:// gothamist.com/2007/02/19/gothamist_goes_to_google.php (accessed June 19, 2007).

12. See Teresa Amabile, *Creativity in Context: Update to the Social Psychology of Creativity* (Boulder, CO: Westview Press, 1996).

13. Edward de Bono, *Six Thinking Hats: An Essential Approach to Business Management from the Creator of Lateral Thinking* (Boston: Little Brown, 1985).

14. Howard Gardner, *Frames of Mind: The Theory of Multiple Intelligences* (New York: Basic Books, 1983).

15. Howard Gardner, "Multiple Intelligences After Twenty Years" (paper presented at the American Educational Research Association, Chicago, Illinois, April 21, 2003); Howard Gardner, "Multiple Lenses on the Mind" (paper presented at the ExpoGestion Conference, Bogota, Colombia, May 25, 2005).

16. See Robert Sternberg, "Intelligence, Competence, and Expertise," in *Handbook of Competence and Motivation*, ed. Andrew Elliot and Carol Dweck (New York: Guilford Press, 2007).

17. Betty Edwards, *Drawing on the Right Side of the Brain*, rev. ed. (New York: Putnam's, 1989), xi.

18. Ibid., 7.

19. Ibid., xiv

10. Do We Do Dewey?

1. Harvard Business School, "The Case Method," http://www.hbs.edu/case/.

2. Louis Barnes, C. Roland Christensen, and Abby J. Hansen, *Teaching and the Case Method* (Boston, MA: Harvard Business School Press, 1994). The guide first came out in 1975. Revisions followed every year from 1977 to 1983 and from 1986 to 1994, for sixteen different printings.

3. C. Roland Christensen, "The Discussion Teacher in Action: Questioning, Listening, and Response," in *Education for Judgment: The Artistry of Discussion Leadership*, ed. C. Roland Christensen, David Garvin, and Ann Sweet (Boston, MA: Harvard Business School Press, 1991), 163.

4. Cecil Fraser, *The Case Method of Instruction* (New York: McGraw-Hill, 1931), 4, 8–9.

5. Thomas Kuhn, *The Road since Structure: Philosophical Essays, 1970–1973*, with an autobiographical interview by James Conant and John Haugeland (Chicago: University of Chicago Press, 2000), 255–256.

6. Thomas Kuhn, *The Structure of Scientific Revolutions* (Chicago: University of Chicago Press, 1962), 164–165.

7. Christensen, "The Discussion Teacher in Action," 159–160.

8. See James Conant, *Two Modes of Thought* (New York: Trident Press, 1964), 43–50. Conant's two modes are deductive and inductive: he argues for both as basic to science. Kuhn reports that Conant "first introduced me to the history of science and thus initiated the transformation in my conception of the nature of scientific advance . . . I taught the historically oriented course that Dr. Conant had started . . . " Kuhn, *The Structure of Scientific Revolutions*, xiii.

9. Jay Martin, *The Education of John Dewey* (New York: Columbia University Press, 2002), 65–73. At first Dewey rejected Peirce, but Martin reports that "Peirce became the philosopher who influenced him the most."

10. Louis Menand, *The Metaphysical Club: A Story of Ideas in America* (New York: Farrar, Straus and Giroux, 2001).

11. Martin Wolf, "The Lessons and Challenges for Greenspan's Fed Replacement," *Financial Times*, October 19, 2005.

12. John Dewey, *Democracy and Education: An Introduction to the Philosophy of Education* (New York: Macmillan, 1916), 400.

13. Martin, *The Education of John Dewey*, 200.

14. John Dewey, *Experience and Education* (New York: Macmillan, 1938), 17.

15. Ibid., 73–74.

16. Ibid., 77.

17. J. Christopher Herold, *Mind of Napoleon: A Selection of His Written and Spoken Words* (New York: Columbia University Press, 1955), 223.

18. Carl von Clausewitz, *On War* (New York: Penguin, 1968/1832), 191.

19. Michael Masoner, *An Audit of the Case Method* (New York: Praeger, 1988). Masoner reports that studies of the effectiveness of the case method do not show the case method to develop decision making significantly better than alternative methods.

20. Charles Abernathy and Robert Hamm, *Surgical Intuition: What It Is and How to Get It* (Philadelphia, PA: Hanley & Belfus, 1995).

21. Robin Hogarth, *Educating Intuition* (Chicago: University of Chicago Press, 2001), 243. Of course not all case teachers follow the pure case method—the teacher can substitute as the expert in the professional script and guide students through the case to the right answer. See Bruce Greenwald, "Teaching Technical Material," in *Education for Judgment: The Artistry of Discussion Leadership*, ed. C. Roland Christensen, David Garvin, and Ann Sweet (Boston, MA: Harvard Business School Press, 1991). For a blend of Greenwald's method and the case method, see Donald Hambrick, "Teaching as Leading," in *Researchers Hooked on Teaching: Noted Scholars Discuss the Synergies of Teaching and Research*, ed. Rae André and Peter Frost (Thousand Oaks, CA: Sage Publications, 1997). See also Geoff Easton, *Learning from Case Studies* (New York: Prentice Hall, 1992), 99–100, for explicit advice to seek past examples in answering case questions: "One of the most frequently used sources of inspiration for problem solutions is experience. Having faced similar problems in the past we are often apt to try again the solutions which worked then. . . . A second source of ideas is knowledge of how other people tackle their problems. . . . In addition . . . it is always possible specifically to seek out information about people or organizations facing problems similar to those you are now facing. . . . In general it is the applied social sciences that make use of case studies for training purposes. The applied nature of these disciplines means that they have developed a body of normative principles, strategies and tactics which have proved useful or successful in situations which form their focus of study. These principles, strategies and tactics will therefore form a bank of possible solutions from which you may choose. . . . After all, you should not have to reinvent the wheel each time you face a problem."

22. Sharon Begley, *Train Your Mind, Change Your Brain: How a New Science Reveals Our Extraordinary Potential to Transform Ourselves* (New York: Ballantine, 2007).

23. See Dalai Lama and Howard Cutler, *The Art of Happiness: A Handbook for Living* (New York: Riverhead Books, 1998). As an American psychiatrist, Cutler

translates the Dalai Lama's Buddhist ideas into mental training independent of the physical disciplines of formal meditation, yoga, or martial arts.

24. In spring 2007 the course received the highest student rating among all 218 courses offered that semester.

11. Kennedy Shoots for the Moon

1. Horatio Alger, *From Canal Boy to President* (New York: John R. Anderson and Company, 1881).

2. Napoleon Hill, *The Laws of Success* (Meriden, CT: Ralston University Press, 1928); Norman Vincent Peale, *The Power of Positive Thinking* (Englewood Cliffs, NJ: Prentice Hall, 1955); Anthony Robbins, *Unlimited Power* (New York: Simon & Schuster, 1987). See also Wayne Dyer, *The Power of Intention* (Carlsbad, CA: Hay House, 2004) and Rhonda Byrne, *The Secret* (New York: Atria Books, 2006).

3. Richard Nelson, *The Moon and the Ghetto* (New York: Norton, 1977).

4. Denise Caruso, "Knowledge Is Power Only if You Know How to Use It," *The New York Times*, March 11, 2007.

5. Excerpts from Urgent National Needs, Joint Session of Congress, May 25, 1961, in *Presidential Files* (Boston, MA: John F. Kennedy Library), http://www.jfklibrary.org.

6. Ibid.

7. Robert Seamans, *Project Apollo: The Tough Decisions* (Washington, DC: NASA, 2005).

8. Ibid., 13.

9. Memorandum for Vice President, April 20, 1961, in *Presidential Files* (Boston, MA: John F. Kennedy Library), http://www.jfklibrary.org. The memo had two more items: "4. In building large boosters should we put our emphasis on nuclear, chemical or liquid fuel, or a combination of these three? 5. Are we making maximum effort? Are we achieving necessary results?"

10. Albert Einstein, "Letter to Walter Dallenbach," May 31, 1915, cited in Alice Calaprice, ed., *The Expanded Quotable Einstein* (Princeton, NJ: Princeton University Press, 2000), 233.

Index

Accidental Empires, 81
African sculpture, 145
Aftercare program, 137
Allen, Paul, 80
  Altair contract, 82
  BASIC, 82, 87
  flash of insight, 81, 82, 86
  Intel's 8080 chip, 81, 85
  Microsoft, 82, 87, 88
  PC revolution, 88
  PDP-8 minicomputer, 80
  vision, 83, 84, 85
Altair, 81, 82, 85, 86, 88
AltaVista, 90, 91, 92
Amdahl, 100
American pragmatism, 163–64,
  171–78
American Revolutionary War, 57
analysis and intuition, 34–35,
  46–47, 107

Anderson, Sean, 92
Anthony, Susan B.
  women's suffrage, 117–18
The Anxiety of Influence, 146
Apple, 87
  strategic innovation, 96–98
Applied Imagination, 148
Aristotle, 17–18
The Art of War, 3, 54, 66, 72
artistic creativity, 143–46
Asian military strategy, 7, 66
astronomical objects, categories
  of, 13–14

Bacon, Roger, 18–19
Baker, Ella, 123, 126
  nonviolent civil
    disobedience, 122
  sit-ins, 126–27
Banker to the Poor, 129

BASIC, 80, 82, 85, 87

Bechtolsheim, Andy, 93

Bhagavad Gita, 3, 66

Bhidé, Amar, 110

Bill & Melinda Gates
  Foundation, 133

Blink, 2

Book of Five Rings, 3, 66

brain
  corpus callosum, 27–28
  hippocampus, 32
  intelligent memory, 33–35
  left–right model, 6, 25–35,
    47, 50
  split-brain, 32

brainstorming, 9, 148–51

Brin, Sergey, 89, 152
  data mining, 90–91
  Google, 91–95
  PageRank, 91–92

Brown vs. Board of Education, 121,
    122, 125, 127

Buddha, 67–68
  beginner's mind, 74
  dharma, 70, 71, 76
  enlightenment, 67, 69, 70
  Four Noble Truths, 69, 70, 73
  goal attainment, 75, 76
  karma, 71
  presence of mind, 70, 71, 73

Burns, Lucy, 118

business strategy, 8, 79, 108

callosotomy, 27–28

can-do American spirit,
    172, 177

Catt, Carrie Chapman, 117–18,
    119, 120

Center For Effective
  Philanthropy, 115

chess players
  decision-making process, 41–42

Columbus legend, 173, 176

Competitive Advantage, 79

Competitive Strategy, 3, 79, 103

Congress for Racial Equality
  (CORE), 127

Consortium for Science, Policy &
  Outcomes, 173

contour maps
  in Napoleon's victory, 56, 57

Copernicus, Nicolaus, 11, 12–15,
    17–18, 74, 76

corpus callosum, 27–28

coup d'oeil, 54–59
  flash of insight, 59
  history, examples from, 58
  presence of mind, 58–59
  resolution, 59

creative destruction, 110

creative ideas, 9, 147–49

creativity, 143
  group methods for, 148
  for individuals, 147

Cringely, Robert, 81, 96

data mining, 90, 91

de Bono, Edward, 153

decisive point, 61, 62

Descartes, 18

Dewey, John, 9
  teaching strategies, 159–70

dharma, 70, 71, 72, 74, 76, 86

Digital Equipment Corporation
  (DEC), 80

Discourse on Methods, 18

Douglass, Frederick, 121
Drawing on the Right Side of the Brain, 154

Edwards, Betty, 154–57
Einstein, Albert, 19, 176
Eliot, T. S., 97
enlightenment of Buddha, 67, 69, 70
Evaluation Research, 134
experimental method, 18, 134
expert intuition, 2, 6, 42, 50
    application of, 40–41
    in mathematics, 43
    problem-solving strategy, 45
    at work, 38

firefighter's action, 38
Flaherty, Paul, 92, 93
flash of insight, 1, 2, 19–20, 59
    of Allen, Paul, 81, 82, 86
    of Baker, Ella, 124, 126
    of Brin, Sergey, 94
    of Buddha, 69–70
    of Gates, Bill, 81, 82, 86
    of Gerstner, Lou, 101
    of Jobs, Steve, 97, 98
    of Klein, Gary, 39
    of Kuhn, Thomas, 20
    of Napoleon, 55–57
    of Page, Larry, 91, 94
    of Paul, Alice, 120
    of Yunus, Muhammad, 130
Four Noble Truths, 69, 70, 73

Gance, Abel, 55
Gardner, Howard
    multiple intelligences, 153, 154

Gates, Bill, 80
    Altair contract, 82
    BASIC, 82, 87
    flash of insight, 81, 82, 86
    Intel's 8080 chip, 81, 85
    Microsoft, 82, 87, 88
    PC revolution, 88
    PDP-8 minicomputer, 80
    presence of mind, 82
    resolution, 83
    vision, 83, 84, 85
Gazzaniga, Michael, 29
General Electric (GE), 135, 137
Gerstner, Lou, 99–101
Give Us Credit, 129
Gladwell, Malcolm, 2
Google, 151, 152
    academic citations, 91
    AltaVista, 91
    data mining, 91
    initial public offering (IPO), 88
    internet, 89
    monopoly, 95
    reverse links, 91
    strategic innovation, 89–95
The Google Story, 89
Gordon, Barry, 33
Gothamist, 151
Grameen Bank, 128, 130, 131–32
graphical user interface (GUI), 97
Great Artists Steal, 97
Greensboro sit-ins, 126, 127

Happiness of Life, 144, 145
Harvard case method, 160, 161–63, 166–68
Heisenberg uncertainty principle, 21

Hewlett-Packard (HP), 89
hippocampus, 32
Honeywell, 83, 85, 87

IBM, 87
  strategic innovation, 99–102
The Innovator's Dilemma, 110
Intel's 8008 microprocessor, 80–81
Intel's 8080 chip, 81, 85
intelligent memory, 6, 33–35, 37,
    58–59, 153–54
  for mathematics, 44
  as single mode of thought,
    46–47

James, William, 21
Joan of Arc, 57
Jobs, Steve
  flash of insight, 97, 98
  MacIntosh, 97
  selective stealing, 98
Jomini, Baron Antoine, 105, 115
  strategic planning, 60
  versus von Clausewitz, 75, 83
Judgment Under Uncertainty:
  Heuristics and Biases,
    106–7
juvenile justice system, 137, 140

Kahneman, Daniel, 80, 106
  and behavioral economics, 108
  heuristics, 106–7
Kandel, Eric, 6, 26, 32, 50, 153
karma, 71, 73, 74, 76
Kennedy, John F., 121
  race to moon, 173–76
Kerr, Steve, 136

King, Martin Luther Jr., 120–23
  Montgomery buy boycott,
    123–24
  Greensboro sit-ins, 126, 127
  nonviolent civil
    disobedience, 124
Klein, Gary, 6, 37
Kuhn, Thomas, 6, 12, 15

Lawson, James, 126
left-right model, of brain,
    6, 47, 50
Les Demoiselles d'Avignon, 145
Levy-Agresti, Jerre, 29–30
light cannon
  in Napoleon's victory, 56, 57
long-term memory, 40, 43
Lopez, George, 149
Lübeck sleep study,
    44–45, 47

MacIntosh, 97
Mara, 69, 74
Mathematical Principles of Natural
  Philosophy, 11
Matisse, Henri, 144–45
Microsoft, 87, 88, 95
  monopoly, 88
  PC revolution, 88
  strategic innovation, 80–88
Milner, Brenda, 32, 50
MITS, 81, 82
Montgomery bus boycott, 123,
    124, 127
Moore's law, 83
Motwani, Rajeev, 90
Musashi, Miyamoto, 3

Napoleon Bonaparte's
    coup d'oeil
    American Revolutionary
        War, 57
    contour maps, 56, 57
    Joan of Arc, 57
    light cannon, 56, 57
National American Women's
    Suffrage Association
    (NAWSA), 117–18, 127
National Association for the
    Advancement of Colored
    People (NAACP), 121, 122,
    123, 125
National Union of Women's
    Suffrage Societies
    (NUWSS), 18
Netscape, 90
Newton, Isaac, 11, 16
Nixon, E. D. 122, 123
nonlinear studies, 63

objective point, 61
Ogawa, Seiji, 31, 50
On the Revolutions of Celestial
    Body, 11
On War, 3, 7, 54
Opus Majus, 18
Origin and Evolution of New
    Businesses, 110
Osborn, Alex, 148, 150
Overture, 94, 95

Page, Larry, 152
    academic citations, 91
    AltaVista, 91
    flash of insight, 91, 94

Google, 91–95
Overture program, 95
PageRank, 91–92
presence of mind, 91, 94
PageRank, 91–92
Palo Alto Research Center
    (PARC), 96
Pankhurst, Emmeline, 118
Patton, George, 62
Paul, Alice, 118, 119
    winning strategy, 119–20
PDP-8 minicomputer, 80, 83
Peloponnesian War, 54
Picasso, Pablo, 144
    and African sculpture, 145
planets, 13–14
Poincaré, 19
Pope Gregory, 15
Porter, Michael, 3, 79–80, 103,
    104, 105, 115
pragmatism, 21–22, 163–64,
    171–78
Pragmatism: A New Name for
    Some Old Ways of
    Thinking, 21
The Price of a Dream, 129
professional scripts, 168
progressive education, 160–66
Ptolemy, 14, 21

reverse brainstorming, 150,
    151, 157
The Road Ahead, 80
Roberts, Ed, 83, 85
Robinson, Jackie, 122
Rustin, Bayard, 122, 123
    civil disobedience, 123, 124

Schumpeter, Joseph, 8, 80,
    110, 143
science education, 167
scientific method, 11–12, 18–19,
    134–35
scientific revolution, 11
short-term memory, 33–34, 40
Siddhartha Gautama,
    See Buddha
Simon, Herbert, 41
sleep, effect of
    on mathematics, 44–45
Sloman, Steven, 47
social enterprise, 8, 133, 135
    strategic planning, 115
Southern Christian Leadership
    Conference (SCLC), 125,
    126, 127
Sperry, Roger, 6, 25, 26–27,
    153, 155
split-brain model, 32, 153,
    155, 156
strategic innovation, 79, 95,
    106, 109
    Apple, 96–98
    Google, 89–95
    IBM, 99–102
    Microsoft, 80–88
strategic planning, 60, 67
Strategic Planning Workbook,
    115–16, 117, 128, 140
The Strategy Paradox, 110
*The Structure of Scientific
    Revolutions*, 6, 12, 16
Student Nonviolent Coordinating
    Committee (SNCC), 127
Summary of the Art of War, 60

tactics, 53
Tao, 65, 66, 71
Tao te Ching, 66
teaching strategies of Dewey,
    159–70
theory of change,
    133–34, 135
Toulon strategy of Napoleon,
    55–57
Traf-O-Data, 81, 84
Tzu, Sun, 3, 54, 66, 71, 72

Vise, David, 89, 91, 94
von Clausewitz, Carl, 3, 7, 53
    coup d'oeil, 54–59
    decisive point, 61
    versus Jomini, 75, 83
    nonlinear studies, 63
    objective point, 61

Wagner, 44
Weiss, Carol, 134, 135
Welch, Jack, 135
Welsh, Dennie, 101
what works matrix, 133, 135–37,
    137–40, 157
Wilson, Woodrow, 119, 120
Wired, 98
Women's Social and Political
    Union, 118
working memory, 34

Yunus, Muhammad, 128
    green revolution, 129
    microcredit, 114, 129, 132

Zen, 65, 67